Conflict, Power, and Organizational Change

A capacity for learning, adapting, and changing is an important facet of organizational resilience. What is involved in generative organizational change? Is it an event, a process, or constantly ongoing? What makes organizational change "good" for the organization? Who has the power to decide what is "good" for the organization and its members? How is it decided? What if there is strong disagreement or conflict? How is that handled? What is the role of organizational members and leaders in these discussions? As these questions demonstrate, the triad of change, power, and conflict are intimately linked.

The purpose of this book is to explore the topics of change, power, and conflict as they relate to the experiences of everyday organizational life. It will provide readers the opportunity to reflect critically on their own local experience and involvement in organizations and to glean actionable wisdom for meaningful engagement and impactful contributions to their organization(s) in the present and future.

Conflict, Power, and Organizational Change will be of interest to students, researchers, academics, and professional colleagues interested in the fields of business and organizational studies, especially those wanting to get acquainted with the concepts of change, power, and conflict in contemporary organizational settings.

Deborah A. Colwill is Associate Professor of Educational and Leadership Studies at Trinity International University, USA.

Routledge Focus on Business and Management

The fields of business and management have grown exponentially as areas of research and education. This growth presents challenges for readers trying to keep up with the latest important insights. *Routledge Focus on Business and Management* presents small books on big topics and how they intersect with the world of business research.

Individually, each title in the series provides coverage of a key academic topic, whilst collectively, the series forms a comprehensive collection across the business disciplines.

Culture and Resilience at Work
A Study of Stress and Hardiness among Indian Corporate Professionals
Pallabi Mund

Optimal Spending on Cybersecurity Measures
Risk Management
Tara Kissoon

Small Business, Big Government and the Origins of Enterprise Policy
The UK Bolton Committee
Robert Wapshott and Oliver Mallett

Conflict, Power, and Organizational Change
Deborah A. Colwill

Human Resource Managementfor Organisational Change
Theoretical Formulations
Dr. Paritosh Mishra, Dr. Balvinder Shukla and Dr. R. Sujatha

For more information about this series, please visit: www.routledge.com/Routledge-Focus-on-Business-and-Management/book-series/FBM

Conflict, Power, and Organizational Change

Deborah A. Colwill

Routledge
Taylor & Francis Group

NEW YORK AND LONDON

First published 2022
by Routledge
605 Third Avenue, New York, NY 10158

and by Routledge
2 Park Square, Milton Park, Abingdon, Oxon, OX14 4RN

Routledge is an imprint of the Taylor & Francis Group, an informa business

© 2022 Taylor & Francis

The right of Deborah A. Colwill to be identified as author of this work
has been asserted by her in accordance with sections 77 and 78 of the
Copyright, Designs and Patents Act 1988.

Library of Congress Cataloging-in-Publication Data
Names: Colwill, Deborah A., author.
Title: Conflict, power, and organizational change / Deborah A. Colwill.
Description: New York, NY : Routledge, 2022. | Series: Routledge focus on
    business and management | Includes bibliographical references and index.
Identifiers: LCCN 2021022411 (print) | LCCN 2021022412 (ebook) |
    ISBN 9780367340995 (hbk) | ISBN 9781032126630 (pbk) |
    ISBN 9780429323959 (ebk)
Subjects: LCSH: Organizational change. | Organizational behavior. |
    Organizational resilience.
Classification: LCC HD58.8 .C6437 2022 (print) | LCC HD58.8 (ebook) |
    DDC 658.4/06—dc23
LC record available at https://lccn.loc.gov/2021022411
LC ebook record available at https://lccn.loc.gov/2021022412

ISBN: 978-0-367-34099-5 (hbk)
ISBN: 978-1-032-12663-0 (pbk)
ISBN: 978-0-429-32395-9 (ebk)

DOI: 10.4324/9780429323959

Typeset in Times New Roman
by Apex CoVantage, LLC

To Jim, Alden, Bobby, Love, Duane, Muriel, Peter, Therese, David, and the BU Cohort. Thank you for your encouragement and support along the way.

Contents

1 The Confluence of Conflict, Power, and Change

Introduction

Chapter 1 introduces and underscores the need to take a look closer at the confluence of conflict, power, and change in organizational life. The chapter begins with two stories that illustrate the interconnected relationship of conflict, power, and change. Next, the triad of conflict, power, and change is explored by asking some probing questions that emphasize the connection. Finally, an overview of the book is offered in which each of the remaining chapters is briefly described.

Two Stories

Throughout my lifetime, I have listened to many organizational members and leaders share stories about their experiences of conflict, power, and change in organizations. Two of these stories begin this introductory chapter.

The newly hired CEO of a financially struggling company called a "Town Hall Meeting" and used the power of his positional authority to mandate significant realignments and budget cuts in the organization. This change declaration was made with little consultation from organization leaders, mid-level managers, or staff. The speech was short and minimal detail given; however, the areas impacted by the directed change were sizable in scope. His change announcement created numerous detrimental unintended consequences. In the aftermath, great confusion arose among managers and employees since little information was provided to guide them. Dysfunctional conflict erupted over who was to lead the effort and how it should be managed. And the resulting cloud of doubt and fear dampened morale among the employees.

A second scenario (in a different organization) happened when a conflict arose between two employees over the interpretation of an organizational policy. The discussion quickly escalated and became heated. Their manager

DOI: 10.4324/9780429323959-1

heard the shouting and called them in to her office. She led them through a process in which the employees discussed and cooled their interpersonal conflict which had nothing to do with the policy dispute. As the conversation cooled, the manager shifted the topic to the policy disagreement. With the anger and anxiety dialed down, they were able to mutually clarify the issue and suggest improvements, which led to changing the policy, and the net result benefited all the employees.

These stories illustrate the interconnected relationship of conflict, power, and change. While the first story is based on a real case of a new and inexperienced CEO, the themes of the story are common. Inexperienced leaders often underestimate the difficulty of navigating the complex dynamics of conflict, power, and change on the organizational road. A related theme happens when leaders overestimate their ability to lead directed change and minimize the input of colleagues in the system which results in harmful unintended consequences. In contrast, the second story depicts a seasoned leader who skillfully navigates the waters of conflict, power, and change with an emphasis on honoring human dignity and the common good. This second story illustrates another common theme, humble savvy leaders find productive ways to manage the situational pressure points and encourage life-giving growth of individuals, teams, and organizations. Stories like these are the catalyst to dive deep into the triad of conflict, power, and change.

Conflict, Power, and Change

Organizations experience many types of challenges and ongoing turbulence. In the face of these challenges, organizational resilience is fostered by intentional learning and adapting. In order to survive, let alone thrive, organizations must learn to skillfully navigate change. Although each of us has witnessed organizational change efforts that have fizzled out or have done more harm than good, organizational change can be leveraged to promote life-giving organizational health. But given that many change efforts are disappointing, how is generative organizational change different? What is the focus of this type of change? Who is involved and how are they involved? And how do organizational members learn, grow, and develop their change capacity both individually and collectively?

Alongside of these questions about the essence of generative change are even more fundamental questions to consider. For example, at the most basic level, what is organizational health? How is organizational health defined or described? Who decides what constitutes organizational health? Who determines what is "good" for a particular organization and what needs changing in the organization? Notice that these questions raise awareness that the act of framing the direction and scope of change is embedded with organizational power. If this is so, then the question must be asked, who holds the power to decide what is "good" for the organization and its members? And what should be changed? Who has a seat at that table and who does not? More broadly, what forms of power exist in organizations? How is power used or abused in organizational life? Can there be honest and transparent discussions of the use of power within organizations? Can power be used for good?

Whether overtly acknowledged or not, organizational change efforts are embedded with power. Navigating who has the opportunity to contribute or lead discussions on the direction and implementation of organizational change is vital, but how these discussions are conducted cannot be overlooked. What is the role of organizational members and leaders in these discussions? What style of communication is used? Who articulates the questions to be engaged? What happens if people are unwilling to speak up with crucial information? Do organizational members feel safe to raise dissenting opinions? What if disagreements are avoided out of fear? Or what if there are strong heated disagreements? How are they handled? Conflict is inevitable in organizational life, especially during times of organizational change. How conflict is viewed and specifically practiced in organizations is crucial.

Conflict, power, and change are intimately linked in organizational life. The abovementioned questions articulated point to the inseparable confluence of this triad. The purpose of this book is to explore the topics of conflict, power, and change as they relate to the everyday life of organizational members and leaders. This book should be of interest to students and professional colleagues who want to get acquainted with the concepts of conflict, power, and change in contemporary organizational settings. The hope is that this book will provide readers the opportunity to reflect critically on their own local experience and involvement in organizational life and to glean actionable wisdom for meaningful engagement and impactful contributions to their organization(s) in the present and future.

Overview of the Book

As the title denotes, the main topics of the book are conflict, power, and change. In order to set the stage for what is ahead, a brief description of the remaining chapters appears in the following paragraphs.

Chapter 2 emphasizes three points of focus needed for navigating conflict, power, and change in organizations. These points of focus are framed using the metaphors of balcony, road, and moorings. These framing metaphors are later used to shape each of the topical chapter discussions on conflict, power, and change. However, Chapter 2 describes the framing metaphors themselves. The first point of focus is observing the organizational landscape from the balcony. The view from the balcony involves contemplating apt theoretical models, honing big picture observational capacities, and asking penetrating reflective and contextual questions. The second point of focus is navigating the terrain along the organizational road. The view along the road examines daily activities, relational interactions, and situational pressures of the organizational members and leaders. The third point of focus is appreciating the significance of organizational moorings. Focus on moorings involves an awareness of and active engagement in shared values and identity that hold the organization steady during turbulent times. The advantages and disadvantages of each of these points of focus will be explored. The chapter will conclude by reflecting on the benefit of holding these points of focus in creative tension.

The third chapter focuses on conflict in organizational life. The flow of the chapter moves from the balcony view, to life on the road, and finally to organizational moorings. On the balcony, a brief background and description of organizational conflict will be offered, followed by a discussion on sources of conflict, a description of conflict styles, and the last balcony topic is leadership, culture, and conflict. The on-the-road aspects explored include counting the costs of dysfunctional conflict and reaping the benefits of productive conflict. The road view also looks at practicing healthy conflict by intentionally managing oneself, deliberately focusing on relationships, and carefully cultivating conversations. The final topic on the road explores cooling the conversation through generative dialogue. Organizational moorings needed to anchor the use of conflict in organizations are discussed: valuing interpersonal relationships and valuing psychological safety. The chapter closes with discussion questions to consider and a brief case study to engage on the topic.

Chapter 4 focuses on the use of power in organizations. The framing of the chapter aligns with the balcony, road, and moorings perspectives. The balcony explores the influence of early writings on power as coercion; the four modes of power, that is, power-over, power-to, power-from, and power-with; and the difficulty of defining power. The balcony view also looks at managers' assumptions and motivations in the use of power as well as cultural power dynamics. The on-the-road aspects we will explore include the social bases of power; the deliberate use of position power and personal power; and some common tactics and practices of power. Organizational moorings needed to anchor the use of power in organizations are discussed: valuing human dignity and valuing trustworthy character. The chapter closes with discussion questions and a brief case study.

Chapter 5 focuses on change in organizations. The chapter's framing moves from the balcony, to the road, and to organizational moorings. The balcony explores four organization archetypes that provide insight on the evolution of organizations. The archetypes are described using four metaphors. Understanding these archetype organizations gives background to explore a variety of organizational change theories and models. The view on the road examines the impact of these archetypes on the roles of organizational leaders and members. Two essential elements for organizational change are discussed: ability and willingness. The relationship between resistance and change is explored, followed by some of the common pitfalls in leading change. The last road topic is managing transitions during change. The organizational mooring perspectives explored are valuing life-giving organizational purpose and creating mutually shared organizational values. Discussion questions and a brief case study close the chapter.

Chapter 6 brings the triad of conflict, power, and change together. Prior chapters have pointed to the fact that conflict, power, and change are everyday aspects of organizational life. Yet, how they are engaged and experienced differ greatly depending on the context and ethos of the organization. Many settings could be used to illustrate the dynamic interaction of conflict, power, and change. The aim of this chapter is to illustrate the interconnections of conflict, power, and change in two different organizational climates: a controlling climate and a trusting climate. The primary reason for choosing these two climates is to highlight the contrast and emphasize the wide range of possible behaviors and impacts that exist with respect to the confluence of conflict, power, and change in organizations. The two illustrative organizational climates will be unpacked using three arenas of organizational involvement: individual employee capacity, people working together, and the situational pressures of organizational life. In summary, with a view toward understanding the interconnections of conflict, power, and change, three arenas of involvement will be explored within controlling climates and trusting climates.

2 Three Points of Focus

Introduction

Chapter 2 emphasizes three points of focus needed for navigating conflict, power, and change in organizations. The points of focus are framed by using the metaphors of balcony, road, and moorings. These framing metaphors are later used to shape each of the topical chapter discussions on conflict, power, and change. However, this chapter will describe the framing metaphors themselves. The view from the balcony involves gaining insight into the organizational system through contemplating helpful theoretical models, honing big picture observational capacities, and asking reflective and contextual questions. The view along the road focuses on the daily activities, relational interactions, and situational pressures of the organizational members and leaders. Focus on moorings involves an awareness of and active engagement in shared values that hold the organization steady during turbulent times. The advantages and disadvantages of each of these points of focus will be explored. The chapter will conclude by reflecting on the benefit of holding these points of focus in creative tension.

Metaphors Illuminate

A primary task of leadership is framing the focus of an organization. Framing focus implies drawing attention to what is important but also removing unwanted distractions that waste time and energy. This chapter explores three points of focus needed for navigating conflict, power, and organizational change. These points of focus will be described through the framing lenses of three metaphors: balcony, road, and moorings.

Why use metaphors to frame focus? Metaphors draw analogies between the features of two unrelated entities in order to suggest a resemblance. They help to frame focus in that: (1) metaphors have the capacity to illuminate new insights about what is familiar to us as well as open up and clarify what is

DOI: 10.4324/9780429323959-2

unfamiliar to us, (2) metaphors focus attention by depicting images that can guide perception and action, and (3) metaphors provide a catalyst to surface and name tacit knowledge (Colwill 2010). While the first two purposes for using metaphors are reasonably clear, the third one may need some explaining. The idea of tacit knowledge simply means that "we know more than we can tell" (Polanyi 1966, 4). For example, "We know a person's face, and can recognize it among a thousand, indeed among a million. Yet, we usually cannot tell how we recognize a face we know. So most of this knowledge cannot be put into words" (ibid., 4). Tacit knowledge is something that we know but cannot put into words. Consequently, "Through metaphor people are better able to put into words tacit knowledge that might be otherwise difficult to access" (Colwill 2010, 116). A caution should be noted. Metaphors are "filters that screen some details and emphasize others" (Barrett and Cooperrider 1990, 222). In other words, "metaphors paradoxically expand one's perspective while at the same time limit the scope of what is seen" (Colwill 2010, 115).

With this background information in mind, we will explore three points of organizational focus via the metaphors of balcony, road, and moorings. While each is depicted separately, it must be said that the power of these metaphors comes in holding them in a creative tension and paying deliberate attention to all three.

Observing the Landscape From the Balcony

The impact of a balcony view is impressive whether it is a twinkling city skyline, a colorful Rocky Mountain sunset, or a picturesque ocean view. The balcony view allows one to step back at a distance and gain a wider perspective of the landscape. From the balcony, we watch, observe, ask questions, reflect, and gain perspective about traveling on the road. Gaining this perspective requires intentionally stepping away from the day-to-day activity of the road to reflect on the bigger picture.

The Balcony and Organizational Life

The view from the organizational balcony involves gaining insight into the organization's system through contemplating helpful theoretical models, honing big picture observational capacities, and asking reflective and contextual questions. Each of these balcony perspectives will be briefly introduced in the following text.

From the balcony, unpacking various theoretical models can provide fresh eyes to examine organizational practice. However, some are quick to point out that a gap exists between the worlds of theory and practice (Van de Ven 2007; Wasserman and Kram 2009). More specifically, "Academics and practitioners dwell in different types of cultures, respect different types of expert knowledge, have different end products in mind, and in essence speak different languages" (Colwill 2012, 24). Yet, a growing tribe of boundary spanning individuals identify with the call to concurrently generate new knowledge and improve practice; they serve as translators to bridge the worlds of theory and practice (Wasserman and Kram 2009; Colwill 2012). For example, "reflective practitioners" use wisdom drawn from on-the-ground seasoned experience augmented by technical expertise to promote effective action in the "swampy zones of practice" (Schon 1987, 3). Another type of boundary spanning activity is "engaged scholarship" where researchers partner with practitioners to gather knowledge that can be used toward innovative organizational practice (Van de Ven 2007).

Spanning the boundaries of theory and practice on the balcony allows leaders and organizational members to reflect on various theoretical models with the possibility of opening up new frames of reference for use on the organizational road. For example, Bolman and Deal (2017, 15) "consolidate major schools of organizational thought and research into a comprehensive framework encompassing four perspectives." The "four frames" they suggest are "structural, human resource, political, and symbolic" (ibid., 16). Exposure to these competing organizational frames fosters a view from the balcony that may challenge old ways of thinking and insert new ways of seeing the landscape that have not been explored before. The new insights gleaned from theory may provide help in navigating conflict, power, and change in organizations.

A second balcony perspective involves honing observational capacities in order to gain insight into the organizational system. Observational capacities take many forms. One example comes from Heifetz and Linsky (2002, 53) who speak about "getting on the balcony" above the "dance floor" to notice patterns within the system that one might overlook without this perspective. Without the balcony perspective, "you are likely to misperceive the situation and make the wrong diagnosis, leading you to misguided decisions about whether and how to intervene" (ibid., 53). Astute observational capacity from the balcony also involves regularly scanning the external environment of the organizational system to monitor for threats, changes, trends, etc. Worley, Williams, and Lawler (2014, 27) name this skill as "perceiving" which is one of the four "routines of agility." According to these authors, perceiving is "the process of broadly, deeply, and continuously monitoring the environment to *sense* changes and rapidly *communicate* these perceptions to decision makers, who *interpret* and formulate appropriate responses" (ibid., 27).

A third balcony vantage point involves asking reflective and contextual questions. Bolman and Deal (2017, 14) assert, "Asking the right question enhances the ability to break frames." At a minimum, breaking frames allows for new essential input that may have been missed. To this end, question posing is an artform that leaders need to learn in order to draw out differing or dissenting perspectives. Each of us is limited by our own frames of reference, as such, a balcony view can be strengthened when exercised with others. Divergent perspectives that articulate unique expertise, experience, and background bring vital fresh insights and information which can benefit an organization and its members. Thus, leaders who view and reflect on daily practice from the balcony in cooperation with coworkers have the opportunity to glean needed insight from those who are naming and framing the situation differently. After intense rich balcony dialogue, common points of focus can provide fertile ground for collaboration in the purpose, direction, and action of an organization in its specific context.

Benefits of the Balcony Perspective

The main benefit of balcony view is that it provides a big picture vantage point to make sense of the organizational road. Paying close attention to the activity on the road, making observations, and noticing patterns will proactively benefit reflection and interpretative work from the balcony. Information that is gleaned on the road can be placed in a broader context of the organizational system and its environment.

Carefully observing the activity on the road requires a balcony mindset even while traveling the road. Listening to those on the road offers a wealth of helpful information and feedback to consider on the balcony. Such feedback from the road perspective could come in the form of questions asked, "Why do we always get stuck at this fork in the road?"; observations offered, "After climbing this steep portion of the trail most people need to rest"; proactive thinking, "I found a faster safer route for us to take"; or cautions to be considered, "The bridge ahead becomes very slippery during the winter months." On the balcony, we can share "the collected wisdom of past travelers" (McGrath 1995, 13). When individuals authentically voice different points of view and show respect by listening carefully to one another, shared meaning and language are created that strengthens collective thinking and collaborative action. In the end, creating shared balcony vantage points helps organizational members and leaders to communicate more effectively with one another on the road.

Cautions Regarding the Balcony View

One caution is the assumption that the balcony vantage point affords you all the information you need to make good decisions about what happens on the road. In other words, "Staying on the balcony in a safe observer role is as much a prescription for ineffectuality as never achieving that perspective in the first place" (Heifetz and Linsky 2002, 53). Instead these authors argue, "The challenge is to move back and forth between the dance floor and the balcony, making interventions, observing their impact in real time, and then returning to the action" (ibid., 53).

Skilled judgment relies on "a repertoire of categories and clues, honed by training and experience" (Bolman and Deal 2017, 13). However, another possible downside of a balcony view comes when leaders limit the focus of what is seen on the balcony through the binoculars of their own technical expertise or skilled judgment. Ironically, poor decisions can be made when an expert prematurely jumps to a conclusion by attending to a narrow set of facts, thus "the quality of your judgments depends on the information you have at hand, your mental maps, and how well you have learned to use them. Good maps align with the terrain and provide enough detail to keep you on course" (ibid., 13). All the more reason to foster collaboration on the balcony rather than making it a solo event.

Another balcony caution takes the form of leaders who prefer a "permanently balconized existence" (Mackay 1946, 29). These individuals relish the detached aerial view. This strong preference for the balcony may potentially lead to disengagement with the people and activities on the road. In other words, even when physically present with others on the organizational road, a balcony-preferred individual may choose not to intentionally engage in daily camaraderie and activity. Left unchecked, this lack of engagement may deteriorate into insensitivity to coworkers and detachment from road activities. Common sense tells us that engaging well on the road is crucial to healthy organizational life.

Navigating the Terrain Along the Road

While the balcony provides a panoramic view, the perspective from the road is a detailed up-close view. The road is the place of action and participation. It is where life is lived, dangers are faced, choices are made, and decisions carried out (Mackay 1946). Experiential learning happens on the road.

The Road and Organizational Life

The road perspective centers on the daily activities, relational interactions, and situational pressures of organizational members and leaders. These three road perspectives will be briefly illustrated in the following paragraphs.

An important focus on the road are the daily activities of organizational members and leaders. One example of a road activity is experimenting. Innovative leaders are "willing to let their organizations experiment, iterate, debrief, learn and start the process over again if necessary" (Hill et al.

2014, 32). Leaders foster "learning by discovery, from trial and error, rather than careful, detailed planning" (ibid., 162). These authors state the process of "creative agility" happens in three phases: "pursue, reflect and adjust" (163). Many other examples of day-to-day road activities exist. Each organizational member or leader engages in a range of activities to help the organization fulfill its mission.

A second area of focus on the organizational road are relational interactions between coworkers. We spend many hours of our life interacting with people in our work environments. The people we work with and our relationships with these individuals have a significant impact on us. When there is a lack of harmony or dysfunctional conflict then, it is more difficult to accomplish the work at hand. Therefore, fostering meaningful connections between colleagues is crucial to an organization's ability to thrive. Creating and reinforcing an environment of safety, trust, and collaboration is a necessary leadership practice.

A third essential perspective on the road involves deliberately attuning to the situational pressures of an organization. Life on the organizational road can be hectic and messy. Organizational members and leaders must pay attention to and address the pressure points. All organizations confront some common pressures: negotiating priorities, making time sensitive decisions, delivering product or service on schedule, or adapting under external pressure. However, the multifaceted nature of situational pressures will take different forms depending on the unique factors within an organization.

Advantages of the Road Perspective

The organizational road is the place of involvement and participation where strength and skill are built over time. Knowledge is formed and tested on the road. Mackay (1946) chides the balcony-only dwellers, that you cannot truly know something unless you experience it firsthand on the road. Schon (1987, 13) adds "We should start not by asking how to make better use of research-based knowledge but by asking what we can learn from a careful examination of artistry, that is the competence by which practitioners actually handle indeterminate zones of practice." The organizational road is the place where stamina, knowledge, and skilled artistry are formed and tested. It is also where people have the opportunity to develop deep commitment to their life work, their colleagues, and the mission of their organization.

Vulnerabilities of the Road-Only View

As discussed earlier, a balcony-only view has value but by itself is incomplete; the same could be said for a road-only view. Focusing only on the road provides up-close detail of what is happening locally but neglects the organizational landscape and the broader environment beyond. Senge (2006, 19) states, "When people in organizations focus only on their position, they have little sense of responsibility for the results produced when all positions interact. Moreover, when results are disappointing, it can be very difficult to know why." When traveling on the road, a nuanced view of the organizational system and its environment is needed.

Another related caution to a road-only view is when problems arise in organizations, a common impulse is to act too quickly based on a weak assessment of the situation. Without a more complete understanding of what is occurring in the organizational system, it is difficult to diagnose a local situation correctly. Achieving some distance from the situation through a system-level balcony view is needed to augment the road perspective. Deficient diagnosis weakens the interpretation of the situation which may result in poor decisions and faulty action (Heifetz and Linsky 2002). Conversely, skilled diagnostic work sets the stage for making appropriate interpretations, decisions, and actions.

Appreciating the Significance of Moorings

As noted earlier, the balcony provides a panoramic view, the road affords a detailed up-close perspective, whereas moorings are sturdy structures to which a vessel may be secured during a storm. Rather than being tossed about by the waves, moorings provide a way of anchoring a ship to keep it safe during turbulent weather.

Moorings and Organizational Life

In the same way that moorings are used to secure a ship during heavy storms, in a metaphorical sense, focus on organizational moorings involves an awareness of and active engagement in shared values that hold the organization steady during turbulent times. In other words, shared values give leaders and members a sense of strength and composure especially during stressful situations or seasons. Shared values are what we agree is truly important to a community or organization. Shared values shape "priorities and choices, they influence individual and collective thought and action" (Hill et al. 2014, 102). Moreover, "Values characterize what an organization stands for, qualities worthy of esteem or commitment" (Bolman and Deal 2017, 243). Broadly speaking, shared values are one aspect of organizational culture. Schein and Schein (2017, 2) state that "cultures are learned *patterns of beliefs, values, assumptions, and behavioral norms that manifest themselves at different levels of observability*." Understanding, articulating, and living out the unique shared organizational values provide strong moorings for its members and leaders.

Benefits of Organizational Moorings

As mentioned previously, organizational moorings can give leaders and members a sense of stability, strength, and composure amid stressful turbulent times. They may also instill a sense of direction and guidance. Bolman and Deal (2017, 421) state, "Organizations need leaders who can provide a durable sense of purpose and direction, rooted deeply in values and the human spirit." They add, "The values that count are those an organization lives, regardless of what it articulates in mission statements or formal documents" (ibid., 243).

Potential Misuse of Organizational Moorings

An organization's moorings or shared values serve to guide, direct, and protect. However, if shared values become too rigid, codified, or fixed, then a potential danger exists. If values become calcified, they function more like an obstacle that inhibits health or growth. Isaacs (1999, 350) illustrates this danger by saying, "Corporate vision statements lock in attitudes, keeping the company from being alive to the ever-changing realities of the market. Heavily ideal-led systems seem to have a great tendency to get paralyzed by their own ideals." He goes on to say, "The problem is not ideals, per se, but the way we think of them. The ecology of our thought—the inherited network of ways of thinking, speaking, and acting in the world—induces us to make idols out of our ideas" (ibid., 352). Idols are "images that we have accepted, that blind or limit us to other possibilities" (354). Isaacs observes, "Many of us develop partial understandings that we see as complete. . . . The more certain we feel of them, the more they limit our freedom to think. We may have spent years building up these certainties, and beneath the fear of letting go of them is indeed the fear of having nothing underneath" (356). Yet, Isaacs adds a word of hope, "The overall problem of certainty can be remedied with an awareness of the motion of change" (356). Could it be that Isaacs is asking us to break up hardened ill-serving ideals and turn toward what is dynamic and life-giving? Having robust honest dialogue about what really matters (i.e., mutually held shared values) may be a way forward.

Holding the Metaphors in Creative Tension

This chapter has explored three points of focus needed for navigating conflict, power, and change in organizations. The metaphors of balcony, road, and moorings represent important points of organizational focus. While each is depicted separately, it must be said that the power of these metaphors comes in holding them in a creative tension and paying deliberate attention to all three. What happens when one perspective of organizational focus is missing?

How might an organization look that neglected the balcony view? The focal points of the road and moorings without a balcony perspective may result in poor diagnosis, weak interpretation, and faulty action due to the lack of system-level awareness. The organization might stagnate or get stuck without the ability to see its own big picture landscape or to scout from the balcony for new growth opportunities. Likewise, there would also be no one scanning the environment for impending threats to the organization.

How might an organization look that paid insufficient attention to the road? The road is daily organizational life: activities, relationships, and pressures. Neglecting what is happening on the road would lead to an organization's deterioration. Through lack of attention, the essential practices and processes would likely become disorganized, ineffective, or unproductive. Organizational members and leaders probably would be frustrated with the disarray and may disengage. This might lead to increasing employee turnover and customer dissatisfaction.

How might an organization look that neglects, minimizes, or completely ignores moorings? Organizational moorings are the shared values that we use to guide, direct, and protect us through focusing us on what is important. Without moorings as an accountable organizational focus, unethical decisions and actions could ensue, unsafe procedures or practices may occur, and people in the organization may be mistreated through a variety of means

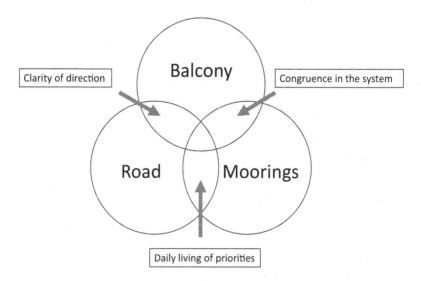

Figure 2.1 Creative tension of balcony, road, and moorings.

such as overworking, underpaying, or systematically inculcating a climate of fear.

A sobering reality is painted in these scenarios. If one of the focal perspectives is missing, then organizations are missing crucial observations, insights, wisdom, collaboration, and action. All three points of focus are needed for navigating conflict, power, and change in organizations. Figure 2.1 illustrates the creative tension that happens when you hold balcony, road, and moorings together in practice.

The interaction of the balcony and the moorings brings congruence in the system. The interaction of the balcony and the road gives clarity of direction. The interaction of the moorings and the road helps us navigate the daily living of our priorities. Some good news is that when allowed to repeatedly guide perception and action, metaphors may in a sense become "self-fulfilling prophecies" (Lakoff and Johnson 1980, 146). The hope is that if organizational members and leaders are able and willing to strengthen each of these points of focus, organizations can increasingly move forward in their mission and toward the common good of all.

References

Barrett, Frank J., and David L. Cooperrider. 1990. "Generative Metaphor Intervention: A New Approach for Working with Systems Divided by Conflict and Caught in Defensive Perception." *The Journal of Applied Behavioral Science* 26 (2): 219–39. https://doi.org/10.1177/0021886390262011

Bolman, Lee G., and Terrence E. Deal. 2017. *Reframing Organizations: Artistry, Choice, and Leadership*. 6th ed. Hoboken: Wiley.

Colwill, Deborah A. 2010. "The Use of Metaphor in Consulting for Organizational Change." In *Consultation for Organizational Change*. Edited by Anthony F. Buono and David W. Jamieson, 113–35. Charlotte: Information Age Publishing.

———. 2012. *Educating the Scholar Practitioner in Organization Development*. Charlotte: Information Age Publishing.

Heifetz, Ronald A., and Marty Linsky. 2002. *Leadership on the Line: Staying Alive Through the Dangers of Change*. Boston: Harvard Business Review Press.

Hill, Linda A., Greg Brandeau, Emily Truelove, and Kent Lineback. 2014. *Collective Genius: The Art and Practice of Leading Innovation*. Boston: Harvard Business Review Press.

Isaacs, William. 1999. "The Perils of Shared Ideals." In *The Dance of Change*. Edited by Peter Senge, 350–57. New York: Currency.

Lakoff, George, and Mark Johnson. 1980. *Metaphors We Live By*. Chicago: University of Chicago.

Mackay, John A. 1946. *A Preface to Christian Theology*. New York: Macmillan Company.

McGrath, Alister E. 1995. *Suffering and God*. Grand Rapids: Zondervan.

Polanyi, Michael. 1966. *The Tacit Dimension*. New York: Doubleday.

Schein, Edgar H., and Peter A. Schein. 2017. *Organizational Culture and Leadership*. 5th ed. Hoboken: Wiley.

Schon, Donald A. 1987. *Educating the Reflective Practitioner: Toward a New Design for Teaching and Learning in the Professions*. San Francisco: Jossey-Bass.

Senge, Peter M. 2006. *The Fifth Discipline: The Art and Practice of The Learning Organization*. Updated ed. New York: Doubleday.

Van de Ven, Andrew H. 2007. *Engaged Scholarship: A Guide for Organizational and Social Research*. New York: Oxford University Press.

Wasserman, Ilene C., and Kathy E. Kram. 2009. "Enacting the Scholar-Practitioner Role: An Exploration of Narratives." *Journal of Applied Behavioral Science* 45 (1): 12–38. https://doi.org/10.1177/0021886308327238

Worley, Christopher G., Thomas Williams, and Edward E. Lawler III. 2014. *The Agility Factor: Building Adaptable Organizations for Superior Performance*. San Francisco: Jossey-Bass.

3 Conflict

Introduction

Conflict can be divisive and destructive or conflict can generate energy and productivity. We have all seen the impact of dysfunctional workplace conflict and the cost that is incurred to employees, teams, and organizations. By contrast, healthy conflict has the capacity to deepen relationships, promote collaboration, enhance performance, improve decision-making, and stimulate innovation. What makes the difference? In organizations, what factors contribute to dysfunctional conflict and what fosters productive conflict? This chapter will look at conflict from the balcony, the road, and organizational mooring perspectives.

Views From the Balcony

The balcony provides a big picture vantage point. As such, the balcony view will describe some crucial concepts on organizational conflict from the literature. To begin, a brief background and description of organizational conflict will be offered, followed by a discussion of conflict sources, and a description of conflict styles. Finally, the last balcony topic explores leadership, culture, and conflict.

Background on Organizational Conflict

Within workplace settings, conflict is often viewed as something to avoid, overcome, or mitigate. Rahim (2015, 13) observes that "classical organization theorists implicitly assumed that conflict was detrimental to organizations, and, as a result, they attempted to eliminate it by designing mechanistic or bureaucratic organization structures." Conflict was thought to be problematic because it impaired the efficiency and effectiveness of organizational systems. Therefore, conflict resolution implied "reduction, elimination, or termination of conflict" (ibid., 45).

DOI: 10.4324/9780429323959-3

By contrast, some contemporary organization theorists see conflict in a more constructive light. Conflict does not always imply dysfunction. And rather than seeking to eliminate conflict, the focus is on managing conflict toward the benefit of the organization and its members. Whereas early theorists focused on conflict resolution, many contemporary theorists focus on conflict management (Rahim 2015). In short, managing conflict requires reducing the dysfunctional aspects of conflict and harnessing the productive aspects of it.

What Is Organizational Conflict?

Pondy (1967, 319) observes, "conflict within an organization can be best understood as a dynamic process underlying a wide variety of organizational behaviors." Framing conflict in this simple neutral way underscores it is an everyday ordinary part of organizational life. Organizational conflict takes place within the context of relationships. At the heart of conflict are actual or perceived differences, disagreements, incompatibilities, or dissensions between individuals, groups, or organizations (Rahim 2015; Zhao, Thatcher, and Jehn 2019). People may choose to disagree about the organization's goals, strategy, processes, alignment, assignments, use of resources, etc. Disagreements may also occur due to personality clashes or conflicting "desires, interests, beliefs, or values between individuals" (Zhao, Thatcher, and Jehn 2019, 112). Behavioral manifestations of conflict may then ensue from these disagreements. Conflict management "refers to behaviors that regulate disagreements (actual or perceived) in groups" (ibid., 115).

Organizational conflict manifests itself in at least three broad behavioral models. The "bargaining model" is "conflict among interest groups in competition for scarce resources" (Pondy 1967, 297). Competitive behaviors are the focus of this model. In the "bureaucratic model" conflict occurs "along the vertical dimension of a hierarchy" (ibid., 297). Control tactics are the aim of this model. The "systems model" is "directed at lateral conflict" (298). Lateral coordination behaviors are the focus of this model. In summary, the central behaviors of these three organizational conflict models are competition, control, and coordination.

Another practical view of how conflict manifests itself in organizations was offered by Follett ([1925] 2013, 31) who states there are "three main ways of dealing with conflict: dominance, compromise or integration." Follett argues, "Domination, obviously, is a victory of one side over the other. This is the easiest way of dealing with conflict, the easiest for the moment but not usually successful in the long run" (ibid., 31). Domination uses competition and control to win the conflict battle. Compromise "is the way we settle most of our controversies; each side gives up a little in order to have peace" (31). Neither side of the argument fully gains what they want and this leaves some unmet desires for both parties. If these unmet desires are important, then they will resurface again in conflict. Follett states, "Compromise does not create, it deals with what already exists; integration creates something new" (35). Integration is a third way of handling conflict in organizations. When the desires of both parties are integrated, that means there is a creative solution in which "neither side has had to sacrifice anything" (32). Integration frees the parties from being stuck "within the boundaries of two alternatives which are mutually exclusive" and reframes the win-lose conflict toward inventing an option that fully encompasses both parties' desires (33). Follett warns "I do not think integration is possible in all cases" (36). The hard work of integration is time-consuming and entails building trust among coworkers as they work toward mutual benefit.

Sources of Conflict

Sources of conflict have been described in a variety of ways. For example, Rahim (2015, 19) names two sources of conflict as "substantive" and "affective." Substantive conflict "is caused by difference of opinion regarding task, policies, procedures, and other business-related or content issues"; differing options are evaluated based on evidence, logic, and critical thinking (ibid., 19). Affective conflict is "associated with personal attacks and criticisms that lead to hostility, distrust, and cynicism" (19). Affective conflict may also be "created by personality clashes" (19).

A similar framework is task conflict and relationship conflict. Edmondson and Smith (2006, 6) state, "Task conflict is conceptualized as differences in opinion relating to work or business decisions, while relationship conflict pertains to personality differences and interpersonal tensions." Moreover, "Moderate levels of task conflict are associated with greater creativity and better outcomes, while relationship conflicts are associated with reduced productivity and morale" (Raines 2020, 226). Relationship conflict is "associated with negative impacts on the team's ability to accomplish its tasks" (ibid., 226).

Conflict Styles

Kilmann and Thomas (1977) built a five-style conflict model adapted from the work of Blake and Mouton (1964). Kilmann and Thomas model is based upon two separate dimensions: "cooperation (attempting to satisfy the other person's concerns) and assertiveness (attempting to satisfy one's own concerns)" (ibid., 38). The five styles are described as follows: "competing is assertive and uncooperative, collaborating is assertive and cooperative, avoiding is unassertive and uncooperative, accommodating is unassertive and cooperative, and compromising is intermediate in both cooperativeness and assertiveness" (38). Self-knowledge about one's conflict style is key to productive conflict management. However, if a leader primarily uses one or two default conflict styles, their unconscious response may not appropriately meet the need of the situation. Whereas "competent conflict managers are adept at analyzing problems and consciously choosing the style most likely to produce the desired results" (Raines 2020, 18). The five styles are briefly described in the following paragraphs.

Conflict avoidance "occurs when an individual or group has evidence that a problem currently exists or will soon exist, but no steps are taken to address the problem" (ibid., 20). Also known as "suppression," the avoiding style often sidesteps or refuses to publicly acknowledge the issue in question (Rahim 2015, 28). Those who avoid conflict may withdraw and delay dealing with the problem, but this may make the situation worse in the long run. The avoiding style may not be appropriate if it is your formal responsibility to resolve the issue; if the issue itself needs prompt attention; or if the issue has great importance to you (Rahim 2015). While the avoiding style is often painted in a negative light, one may intentionally choose this style if the problem is insignificant or temporary; if the "potential dysfunctional effect of confronting the other party outweighs benefits of resolution"; or if a "cooling off period is needed" (ibid., 52).

The accommodating style is "unassertive and cooperative" (Kilmann and Thomas 1977, 38). Accommodating occurs when one party sacrifices their preferred outcome so that the other party may realize their outcome. Palmer (2020, 26) states the "intent" of accommodating is "to preserve, at any cost, the relationships with the group and between opposing parties." This style is also known as "obliging" indicated by "low concern for self and high concern for others" (Rahim 2015, 28). The value of preserving relationships and keeping harmony is important to those who heavily use the accommodating style but this comes with a cost of not fully exploring or valuing the accommodating person's preferred outcomes. This neglect of one party's concerns will likely have consequences in the long term especially if the issue is of great importance to them. Accommodating can be an appropriate approach to conflict "when the issue is relatively insignificant or temporary" (Palmer 2020, 26). This style is often used "when an individual is in a low-power position, with little hope of achieving the preferred outcome" (Raines 2020, 22).

The compromising conflict style seeks a middle ground where each party gives up a little to reach agreement but no one gains all of what they want (Follett [1925] 2013). This style is often used when a temporary solution is needed for an urgent issue, or when "opposing parties of equal strength are stubbornly committed to different goals and solutions" (Palmer 2020, 29). Compromising can yield workable solutions, however it can also encourage "game-playing rather than open and sincere expression of needs, goals, and limitations" (Raines 2020, 24).

The collaborating style seeks to explore conflicts and find points of agreements that go beyond the initial limited view of the problem in order to reach a creative solution that is acceptable to both parties. Follett ([1925] 2013, 31) named this approach "integration." The "integrating style" has "high concern for others and self" (Rahim 2015, 27). Collaborators prefer to work together with others and make joint decisions that achieve outcomes of mutual benefit. They tend to be both "issues-oriented and relationship-oriented" (Palmer 2020, 27). The integrating style is effective when issues are complex and when more than one party is needed to solve the problem. Collaborative colleagues create substantive solutions through the synthesis of their ideas, skills, and resources. The collaborative style should be used when mutual commitment to a decision is needed but this style requires adequate time for input and discussion.

The competing style is "assertive and uncooperative" (Kilmann and Thomas 1977, 38). The competing conflict style "may use smooth diplomacy or raw power" but the ultimate goal is to win the argument (Palmer 2020, 29). Those who favor this style see workplace interactions as "zero-sum" competitions rather than "negotiations that yield joint gains for both parties" (Raines 2020, 25). Competition is their default mode. This style is also known as the "dominating style" which has "low concern for others and high concern for self" (Rahim 2015, 28). A competitive style may be appropriate when time is short and a quick decision needs to be made or "when an unpopular, but necessary, decision must be made by a person in leadership" (Palmer 2020, 30).

People routinely use only one or two conflict styles. A preferred style may be linked to your cultural upbringing, your family of origin, or other life experiences. Self-awareness regarding your preferences and habits will help you improve your conflict responses and may open up your understanding of your colleague's conflict style preferences.

Leadership, Culture, and Conflict

As with language learning, we learn about conflict "by watching and listening to those around us. The way in which we communicate our approach to conflict includes both verbal and non-verbal signals we give to others, either purposefully or subconsciously" (Raines 2020, 27). If conflict is a dynamic process that occurs in everyday life and if we learn about conflict in the same way we learn language, then our cultural roots regarding conflict run deep. Trompenaars and Hampden-Turner (2012, 8) observe that "*culture is the way in which a group of people solves problems and reconciles dilemmas.*" Conflict engagement and culture are closely linked.

In organizations, culture manifests itself on at least three different levels: "national, corporate, and professional" (ibid., 9). These different levels of culture provide filters through which people process their experiences of organizational conflict. Dissonance is created when these different levels of culture clash, yet organizations "cannot strip people of their commonsense constructs or routine ways of seeing. They come to us as whole systems of patterned meanings and understandings. We can only try to understand, and to do so means starting with the way they think and building from there" (24). When engaging workplace conflict, it is crucial to begin by seeking to understand one another and build relational trust. We need to learn one another's unique language of conflict engagement.

Organizational conflict management practices cannot ignore the influence of these three levels of culture. Therefore, "rather than there being 'one best way of organizing,' there are several ways, some much more culturally appropriate and effective than others" (25). Hofstede (1993, 89) argues, "how can we expect one country's theories of management to apply abroad? One should be extremely careful in making this assumption and test it before considering it proven. Management is not a phenomenon that can be isolated from other processes taking place in a society." Expressions of conflict management in organizations may vary considerably depending on underlying cultural values of the organizational leaders and members.

The tone of organizational conflict management is often set by its leaders. Researchers have sought to examine the intersection of culture and leadership. One well-known example is the GLOBE study (House et al. 2004). The acronym GLOBE stands for Global Leadership and Organizational Behavior Effectiveness. This study's intent was "to explore the cultural values and practices in a wide variety of countries, and to identify their impact on organizational practices and leadership attributes" (ibid., 3). Awareness of these leadership attributes is helpful in navigating conflict. However, it has been observed that "The existing literature on cross-cultural management is more useful at the conceptual level than at the behavioral level" (Javidan et al. 2006, 84). One possible reason is that advice at the behavior level is very difficult to pin down due to divergent cultural values embedded within organizations. Although, "different countries do have divergent views on many aspects of leadership effectiveness, they also have convergent views on some other aspects" (ibid., 75). Therefore, "Identifying universally desirable and undesirable leadership attributes is a critical step in effective cross-cultural leadership" (75).

Focusing on the positive attributes provides a starting point to build upon especially during times of organizational conflict. The "universally desirable leadership attributes" identified in the GLOBE study are "trustworthy, dynamic, decisive, intelligent, dependable, plans ahead, excellence oriented, team builder, encouraging, confidence builder, informed, honest, effective bargainer, motive arouser, win-win problem solver, positive, foresight, just, communicative, motivational, coordinator, and administratively skilled" (House et al. 2014, 24). No person embodies all these attributes, but they provide awareness about what to build on and what may need improvement. There will be differences in how these attributes are enacted. The desirable attributes could be good conversation starters within a diverse community to help organizational members understand each other.

Avoiding undesirable leadership attributes is also essential especially when engaged in conflict. These undesirable attributes may exacerbate task or relational conflict. The "universally undesirable leadership attributes" identified in the GLOBE study are "nonexplicit, dictatorial, loner, ruthless, asocial, egocentric, irritable, and noncooperative" (House et al. 2014, 24). Again, one must keep in mind that there may be cultural differences in how leaders enact both the positive and negative leadership attributes. Having good intention is essential, but how behavior is perceived by coworkers is also important. Trusted feedback will help leaders grow, if they listen well, and incorporate the feedback. This is especially true when it comes to managing organizational conflict on the road.

Life Along the Road

On the road, conflict is an inevitable part of organizational life. Liddle (2017, 21) states, "Conflict can be toxic, harmful and destructive. It can also be a powerful driver of change, learning and growth." In short, conflict can be a negative or positive force depending on how it is handled. Additionally, Rahim (2015, 11) notes, "too little conflict may encourage stagnancy, mediocrity and groupthink, but too much conflict may lead to organizational disintegration." However, "a moderate amount of conflict, handled in a constructive manner, is essential for attaining and maintaining an optimum level of organizational effectiveness" (ibid., 11).

Leaders need courage, confidence, and competence to manage conflict well (Liddle 2017). Our "challenge is not to eliminate conflict but to transform it" and "we should not underestimate the difficulty of this task, yet no task is more urgent in the world today" (Fisher, Ury, and Patton 2011, xiii). The view of conflict from the organizational road will focus on the following: counting the costs of dysfunctional conflict, reaping the benefits of productive conflict, practicing healthy conflict, and cooling the conversation through generative dialogue.

Counting the Costs of Dysfunctional Conflict

When something is dysfunctional, it is not operating in an optimal or healthy way. Dysfunctional conflict is "harmful, stressful and costly" and it "generates little, if any, benefit for the parties, their colleagues, or the organization as a whole" (Liddle 2017, 24). Many potential costs or outcomes of dysfunctional conflict exist. Some of the potential costs will be briefly described in subsequent paragraphs at the individual employee level, the work group or team level, and the organizational level.

When employees are involved in dysfunctional workplace conflict (depending on the duration and severity of the conflict), several potential costs can occur that impact the individual organizational member and their contribution to the organization. The first broad area of cost to the individual employee is the impact on their well-being which could include physical and emotional health issues, increased absentee levels, "job stress, burnout, and dissatisfaction" (Rahim 2015, 7). A second cost relates to the employee's work contributions which could include draining time and energy away from essential work tasks, reducing overall job performance, declining employee engagement, reducing motivation to work, and decreasing commitment or loyalty to the organization (Rahim 2015; Liddle 2017).

Dysfunctional conflict has potential costs for work groups or teams as well. One broad area of cost is the potential damage to coworker relationships. Unhealthy conflict can erode trust among team members and break down their ability to communicate. Resentment and unhealthy competition may build up (Palmer 2020). Another conflict cost for teams is the impact on their ability to accomplish their work. Unhealthy conflict can dampen a team's motivation to work together and can reduce productivity levels (Liddle 2017). During dysfunctional conflict, a fight or flight response by team members may escalate and further complicate the issues (Raines 2020). Creativity is stifled when team conflict is too hot; people do not feel safe to share new ideas or dissenting opinions (Edmondson and Smith 2006). Another obvious cost is the amount of time and energy wasted in unhealthy conflict that could be spent in more productive ways.

On the organizational level, many costs are incurred due to dysfunctional conflict. A major cost of dysfunctional conflict for an organization is increased employee turnover (Liddle 2017). The costs involved in employee turnover are not only losing valued and skilled staff, but also recruiting, hiring, and training replacement staff. Dysfunctional conflict may contribute to "a climate of distrust and suspicion" and "resistance to change can increase"

(Rahim 2015, 7). Another potential cost of dysfunctional conflict is "impact on customer experience" and "reputational damage" to the organization (Liddle 2017, 96). In short, "unproductive conflicts and poor management methods hurt the bottom line" (Raines 2020, 10).

Reaping the Benefits of Productive Conflict

Even though many costs are associated with dysfunctional conflict, "the goal cannot and should not be to eliminate conflict. Conflict is an inevitable—and useful—part of life" (Fisher, Ury, and Patton 2011, xiii). Productive conflict "is evidence that people and organizations are alive. It is evidence that people are doing creative thinking and coming up with new ideas and needed changes" (Palmer 2020, 16). Potential benefits of productive conflict will be briefly explored at the individual employee level, the work group or team level, and the organizational level.

When individual employees are involved in productive conflict or negotiation, they may benefit from exercising "a core set of five interests: *autonomy*, the desire to make your own choices and control your own fate; *appreciation*, the desire to be recognized and valued; *affiliation*, the desire to belong as an accepted member of some peer group; *role*, the desire to have a meaningful purpose; and *status*, the desire to feel fairly seen and acknowledged" (Fisher, Ury, and Patton 2011, 32). These five interests can be increasingly affirmed and expressed in healthy conflict and afford organizational members the opportunity to grow. Palmer (2020, 16) agrees that when employees engage in healthy conflict, "it can lead to renewed motivation" and "to personal growth and maturity."

Several potential benefits exist for teams as they interact in healthy conflict. First of all, "Encouraging healthy conflict and learning to deal with it openly in the early stages, fosters confidence in people's ability to face conflict and deal with it in a positive way" (ibid., 19). When teams do the hard work of navigating through their disagreements, their collective confidence to deal with conflict grows as they build trust with one another. Consequently, another important benefit for teams that engage in healthy conflict is building mutual trust. A third potential benefit of engaging in healthy conflict is that teams may grow in their ability to work well together. In productive conflict, team members collaboratively learn from one another and new discoveries are made. Moreover, "positive conflict" allows for "the healthy sharing of differences of opinion and negotiation necessary to make tough decisions" (Raines 2020, 225). Palmer (2020) adds that engaging in healthy conflict provides teams a chance to appropriately vent frustrations in order to clear the air. In short, productive conflict has the potential to enhance group performance (Rahim 2015, 6).

Generally speaking, an "organization that is changing to meet new demands and opportunities, will experience conflict" (Palmer 2020, 19). On the organizational level, many potential benefits accrue from healthy conflict. Raines (2020, 16) argues that "conflict presents an opportunity for positive change, deepening relationships, and problem solving." Rahim (2015, 6) observes several potential outcomes for organizations: "conflict may stimulate innovation, creativity, and change"; "organizational decision-making processes may be improved"; "alternative solutions to a problem may be found"; and "conflict may lead to synergistic solutions to common problems."

Practicing Healthy Conflict

As noted earlier, two common sources of organizational conflict are "substantive conflict" and "affective conflict" (Rahim 2015, 19). Task-related issues are the focus of substantive conflict. Affective conflict is based on "personal attacks and criticisms" as well as "personality clashes" (ibid.,19). It is helpful to be aware of these sources of conflict when considering healthy conflict practices. Many practices could be named; however, three broad areas are explored in the following sections: intentionally managing oneself, deliberately focusing on relationships, and carefully cultivating conversations (Edmondson and Smith 2006).

Intentionally Managing Oneself

Broadly speaking, the first area of healthy conflict practice is intentionally managing oneself. This skill is especially important during affective conflict interactions that can easily become heated. Edmondson and Smith (2006, 12) describe managing self as "the ability to examine and transform the thoughts and feelings that hijack one's ability to reason calmly when conflicts heat up." This is not suppressing emotion, it is *reflecting on their reactions* and *reframing the situation*, thereby becoming less emotionally triggered and more able to ask questions and consider alternative interpretations" (ibid., 13).

Intentional self-management requires the emotional intelligence skills of "emotional expressiveness," "emotional sensitivity," and "emotional control" (Riggio and Reichard 2008, 171). Whereas the skill of "emotional expressiveness is the ability to communicate nonverbally, especially when sending emotional messages, emotional sensitivity refers to skill in receiving and interpreting the nonverbal, or emotional, expressions of others. Finally, emotional control refers to regulating nonverbal and emotional displays" (ibid., 171). These skills are useful in intentionally maintaining a cool posture during heated affective conflict and "conveying positive affect and regard" as well as "establishing rapport" (172).

Deliberately Focusing on Relationships

A second broad area of healthy conflict practice is deliberately focusing on relationships. When engaging workplace conflict, it is crucial to begin by seeking to understand one another and building interpersonal trust. Listening intently to the interests and concerns of all those involved is necessary. This does not imply a heavy accommodating conflict style that capitulates to another parties' demands. Rather it recognizes that healthy interactions with coworkers are essential especially during affective conflict. In other words, "Managers who take the time to get to know each other as people and to understand each other's goals and concerns are less likely to speculate negatively about each other's motives and more likely to ask one another about their concerns. This is how to build trust that is grounded in experience" (Edmondson and Smith 2006, 20).

Conflict "can help or hurt team performance. In some teams it can be a destructive force that damages performance, but in others it can stimulate richer interactions among teammates and improve performance" (Bradley et al. 2012, 156). Riggio and Reichard (2008, 171) name three social intelligence skills that are useful when engaging in conflict, "social expressiveness," "social sensitivity," and "social control." More specifically, "Social expressiveness is ability to communicate verbally and skill in engaging others in social interaction. Social sensitivity is verbal listening skill, but also ability to 'read' social situations, and general knowledge of social rules and norms. Social control refers to sophisticated social role-playing skills and tact in social situations" (ibid., 171). Each of these skills helps us to deliberately focus on our coworkers while in conflict. If colleagues are willing to take the time to work through disagreements in healthy ways, then this may benefit all involved. In other words, "it is not conflict that hurts our relationships—it is the way we approach it, manage it, and communicate it" (Raines 2020, 16).

Carefully Cultivating Conversations

Affective conflict may be calmed by attending to the practices of intentional self-management and deliberate focus on relationships, whereas substantive or task conflict is engaged by carefully cultivating conversations. This involves improving the ways that coworkers communicate about the substantive issues, and their needs and interests. Fisher, Ury, and Patton (2011, 11) assert that when colleagues are engaged in substantive conflict conversations, they should "focus on interests, not positions." When people argue from the standpoint of positions, it often locks them into a zero-sum mindset which sets up a win-lose battle. In short, "positional bargaining puts relationship and substance in conflict" (ibid., 22). Instead, "shared interests and differing but complementary interests can both serve as the building blocks for a wise agreement" (45). Edmondson and Smith (2006) note it is beneficial to explore competing ideas; ask people about what they are thinking and feeling with the goal of understanding what leads them to think and feel this way; reflect on how team member interests intersect with the team's interests; and rely on trustworthy data to make decisions. Elmer (1993, 181) observes "a win-win resolution is possible if both parties can remain calm, understand each other's interests and negotiate with integrity and fairness." When you carefully cultivate conflict conversations, not only does it allow the team to create a wider range of innovative solutions to the common issues they face, team members can also strengthen relationships, and enhance the "team's cooling system" (Edmondson and Smith 2006, 26). This collective capacity to cool the conversation is the focus of the next section on dialogue.

Cooling the Conversation Through Generative Dialogue

Dialogue is a mode of communication that can bring together conflicting parties in a way that cools the conversation and helps those involved to focus on what is most important for the individuals and the common good (Colwill 2005). Building on the three broad abovementioned healthy conflict practices, the mindset and skills of dialogue develop and deepen the collective group experience toward what Follett ([1925] 2013, 31) named as "integration."

What Is Dialogue?

The most elementary understanding of the word "dialogue" stems from the Greek word *dialogos* which means "flow of meaning" and the "image that the derivation suggests is of a *stream of meaning* flowing among and through us and between us. This will make possible a flow of meaning in the whole group, out of which may emerge some new understanding" (Bohm 1996, 6). Flow of meaning or shared meaning is a process of inquiry that happens "*within* and *between* people" (Isaacs 1999, 9). Skilled communication and mutual understanding are necessary for shared meaning to occur in dialogue (Colwill 2005). Ideally, a dialogue group should be a "microculture" of the larger system, representing the multiple views and values of the people (Bohm 1996, 13). Shared meaning is enriched when a diverse interdependent group of people, who respect one another as equals, collaboratively discover and learn together. Dialogue allows a group to go beyond any one individual's understanding of a topic or issue.

Physicist and philosopher, David Bohm, describes another helpful metaphor that unpacks the collaborative cooling nature of dialogue. His studies in physics shed light on human experience. Bohm compared dialogical conversations to the field behavior of a superconductor. Isaacs (1993, 31–32) reports,

> In superconductivity, electrons cooled to very low temperatures act more like a coherent whole than as separate parts. They flow around obstacles without colliding with one another, creating no resistance and very high energy. At higher temperatures, however, they began to act like separate parts, scattering into a random movement and losing momentum. Depending on the environment in which they operate, electrons behave in dramatically different ways.

Metaphorically speaking, the superconductor that holds the electrons is analogous to the "container" for dialogue. When the superconductor is heated, the electrons act like separate parts, colliding with each other, losing energy, and slowing down in their momentum; this resembles heated unhealthy relational conflict where people collide with each other, don't listen to one another, and as a result energy and vitality drain from the parties involved. In contrast, generative dialogue acts like the field behavior of electrons within a cooled superconductor. The "cooling" of the dialogue container happens when people skillfully and collectively practice dialogue together. When dialogue cools the interaction, then flow of meaning gradually begins to take place in the group even if obstacles, issues, or conflicts are introduced into the conversation (Isaacs 1999). People skillfully handle disagreements because they have learned how to coherently think, talk, and act together (Bohm 1996). Individuals gain energy in the process and this enhances and develops the group's cooling system.

On-the-road Practices of Dialogue

Isaacs (1999) identified four basic group practices that are necessary for dialogue to flourish. The practices are respecting, listening, suspending, and voicing. A brief sketch of each practice will appear in subsequent paragraphs.

Respecting is the first dialogue practice. Especially during disagreements, respecting implies treating another person with honor, as a peer whose presence in the group is desired. More than mere goodwill, respecting involves developing a deep admiration of the other person and their views. Genuine respect fuels the development of collegial relationships needed for generative dialogue (Colwill 2005). Isaacs believes that, "Respect is not a passive act. To respect someone is to look for the springs that feed the pool of their experience. The word comes from the Latin *respecere*, which means 'to look again' . . . it involves a sense of honoring or deferring to someone" (Isaacs 1999, 110). Giving people the honor of looking deeper into what is important to them is a clear demonstration of respect.

The second dialogue practice is listening. Edmondson (2019, 199) states, "True listening conveys respect—and in subtle but powerful ways reinforces the idea that a person's full self is welcome here." Listening requires deliberate focused attention on what another is saying, discipline to remain quiet while another is speaking, and asking follow-up questions that draw out the full meaning of the other person (Colwill 2005). When engaged in conflict, it is necessary to frequently acknowledge and summarize what the other person has said to check for trustworthy understanding (Elmer 1993). Furthermore, "As you repeat what you understood them to have said, phrase it *positively* from their point of view, making the strength of their case clear" realizing that "understanding is not agreeing" (Fisher, Ury, and Patton 2011, 37). During times of intense conflict, heated discussions, or problem-solving, participants in dialogue will be aided by genuinely demonstrating active listening with one another: this cools the container.

A third practice of dialogue is suspending judgment, which involves self-control in delaying one's hasty judgments of another person, their opinion, or their behavior (Colwill 2005). Isaacs (199, 141) describes suspension as "the art of loosening one's grip and gaining perspective." Yet, when in conflict, we often make untested assumptions about what motivates people based on limited knowledge of their real concerns. Fisher, Ury, and Patton (2011, 26) warn that when you are embedded in affective conflict, "Don't deduce their intentions from your fears." Broadly speaking then, "The ability to see the situation as the other side sees it, as difficult as it may be, is one of the most important skills a negotiator can possess" (ibid., 25). Therefore, the practice of suspending requires us to "seek understanding through inquiry before forming judgments and making accusations (blaming)" and to "put yourself in the other person's place and try to appreciate his or her perspective on the matter" (Elmer 1993, 181). A skilled dialogue group will practice collective suspension in which they raise to the "surface issues that impact everyone in a way that all can reflect on them" (Isaacs 1999, 155).

The fourth practice of dialogue is voicing. In short, voicing involves speaking authentically about what is important to oneself, yet maintaining an awareness of others and their opinions (Colwill 2005). Voicing requires courage to honestly speak one's thoughts even if the view to be expressed is a dissenting one. Differences of opinion provide wisdom from varying points of view. Another helpful way of describing authentic voicing during times of conflict comes from Alvarez (2017, 151) who states that engaging in "controversy with civility is characterized by a safe and supportive environment of trust, respect, and collaboration" and it "challenges group participants to discuss diverse opinions and perspectives while maintaining respect for other group members and their ideas."

Follett ([1925] 2013, 77) realized the need "to substitute conferring for fighting, to recognize that there are two kinds of difference, the difference which disrupts and the difference which may, if properly handled, more firmly unite." She is speaking of an "integrative unity" or what we have been calling shared meaning. This happens when people with differing opinions turn toward one another in dialogue, and recognize how much they truly have in common (Colwill 2005). In other words, "Dialogue is a *conversation with a center, not sides.* It is a way of taking the energy of our differences and channeling it toward something that has never been created before" (Isaacs 1999, 19).

Practicing dialogue is time-consuming, and therefore not an appropriate mode of communication in every situation, for example urgent decision-making where time is short. However, if organizational members inculcate a dialogue mindset and practices along the way in an everyday sense, as well as set aside concentrated times for deeply engaging in dialogue, then shared meaning and trusting relationships form the basis upon which to accomplish urgent decisions or tasks. Engaging in dialogue, over time, collectively enhances and develops the "cooling system" among coworkers and this will benefit those involved as well as the organization as a whole.

Focus on Organizational Moorings

Organizational moorings are the values that anchor an organization during turbulent times. Two of the many values that could anchor an organization during conflict are valuing interpersonal relationships and valuing psychological safety.

Valuing Interpersonal Relationships

Barrett (2017, 70) simply states, "A basic need for all organizations is to create harmonious interpersonal relationships and good internal communication." When healthy relationships are fostered in organizations, there is a sense of harmony and belonging among employees which directly links to "ensuring customers feel cared for and are happy with your products and services. If harmony cannot be achieved, frictions, frustrations and fragmentation will appear that undermine the organization's performance" (Barrett 2017, 68). Harmonious relationships benefit employees and the organization.

Relationships are formed over time through the interactions people have in their daily communication and activities. While there may be a variety of ways to describe relationships at work, two broad approaches are "transactional role relationships" and "personal relationships" (Schein and Schein 2018, 1). Transactional role relationships rely "on rules, roles, and the maintenance of appropriate professional distance" (ibid., 4). In transactional role relationships, employee interactions are based on what is appropriate and expected for that organization and type of industry. These relationships tend to be formal and restrictively align within the expectations of the role one plays. In contrast, "personal relationships" are "cooperative, trusting relationships as in friendships and in effective teams" (3). A coworker is not merely seen in terms of their role in the organization but as a valued whole person (24). Personal relationships are more suited for organizational contexts that require learning, adaptation, and innovation. In these organizations, "a learning mindset, cooperative attitudes, and skills in interpersonal and group dynamics" are crucial (20).

In a similar fashion, DeRue and Workman (2013, 792) speak about "positive" relationships "in which there is a true sense of mutuality and relatedness, such that people experience mutual giving and receiving, caring, and safety in challenging times." The mutual concern and care expressed in these relationships create openness and trust. Kouzes and Posner (2017, 206) remind us that, "People work together most effectively when they trust one another."

Organizations have a choice as to whether or not they intentionally inculcate the mooring of valuing interpersonal relationships. This requires not just giving lip service to the value of relationships but instead demonstrating the value in action. One challenge "in facilitating relationships is making sure people recognize how much they need one another to excel—how truly interdependent they are" (ibid., 217). Fostering the value of relationships requires creating conditions that promote collaboration. Leaders must "develop cooperative goals and roles, support norms of reciprocity, structure projects to promote joint efforts and encourage face-to-face interactions" (208). Facilitating relationships "implies a deeper level of trust and openness in terms of (1) making and honoring commitments and promises to each other, (2) agreeing to not undermine each other or harm what we have agreed to do, and (3) agreeing not to lie to each other or withhold information relevant to our task" (Schein and Schein 2018, 34). As well as being "sensitive to boundaries of privacy and propriety" (ibid., 34). In short, promoting an organizational climate that values interpersonal relationships is faithfully lived out on a daily basis.

During times of conflict, relationships can be stretched. The strength of a relationship is tested during conflict. Depending on how the conflict is handled, relationship strength can be built or battered. Over time, if conflicts are handled well, trust is built based on experience. Valuing interpersonal relationships is an important mooring for organizations.

Valuing Psychological Safety

Organizational learning is essential to stay adaptive in an ever-changing environment and "psychological safety is foundational to building a learning organization" (Edmondson 2019, 187). The primary reason psychological safety is necessary in learning organizations is that employees need a safe place to learn, share knowledge, and create. Along the way, they need to be able to share "concerns, questions, mistakes, and half-formed ideas" (ibid., xiv). And, if "people don't speak up, the organization's ability to innovate and grow is threatened" (22). What is psychological safety? Broadly speaking, it is "defined as a climate in which people are comfortable expressing and being themselves" (xvi).

Whether consciously or not, most people weigh the interpersonal risks involved in their work relationships (22). In an unsafe environment when employees experience fear, it is unlikely they will speak up even if they are convinced that what they have to say is important (30). Yet, if people remain silent, then their ideas, cautions, and questions are not heard. When people avoid the risk of speaking up, it blocks the learning of coworkers since the information that could have been helpful was not shared.

Some might believe that striking fear within employees may fast-track performance. Bolman and Deal (2017, 36) observe "Fear may bring about compliance, but it never generates commitment." Fear inhibits learning and "for jobs where learning or collaboration is required for success, fear is not an effective motivator" (Edmondson 2019, 14). By contrast, a psychologically safe climate encourages employees to "engage in learning behaviors, such as information sharing, asking for help, or experimenting" (ibid., 14). Moreover, employees "feel comfortable sharing concerns and mistakes without fear of embarrassment or retribution. They are confident that they can speak up and won't be humiliated, ignored, or blamed. They know they can ask questions when they are unsure about something. They tend to trust and respect their colleagues" (xvi).

A climate of "psychological safety is about candor and willingness to engage in productive conflict so as to learn from different points of view" (14). For example, teams with an established climate of psychological safety that engage in task conflict improve their team performance (Bradley et al. 2012). Furthermore, the combination of "psychological safety and task conflict appear to enable teams to generate more creative ideas and critically discuss decisions, without team members getting embarrassed or taking the constructive conflict personally" (ibid., 156). Leaders create the conditions "to ensure that the talent in an organization is able to be put to good use to learn, innovate, and grow. Speaking up is not a natural act in hierarchies. It must be nurtured" (Edmondson 2019, 146). In short, "psychological safety is mission critical when knowledge is a crucial source of value. In that sense, the fearless organization is something to continually strive toward rather than to achieve once and for all. It's a never-ending and dynamic journey" (103). Psychological safety among coworkers is a primary mooring for organizations.

Discussion Questions

- Which topics from this chapter struck a chord with you? How will you put them into practice?
- How would you summarize the difference between relationship conflict and task conflict?
- Which are your preferred styles of engaging in conflict? Tell a story that highlights an example.
- What are the signs of dysfunctional conflict in your context? What costs have you observed?
- How would you describe healthy conflict? What are some of its potential benefits?
- What is the relationship between intentional self-management and team conflict?
- In what ways does working through healthy task conflict build trust among coworkers?
- "If someone said to you, 'Conflict never ends well'"; how would you respond to this statement?
- What is meant by psychological safety? Why is it important for engaging in productive conflict?

The Case of Inherited Team Conflict

Makayla was recently internally promoted to assistant manager for a large retail store. She was assigned to lead an existing cross-functional team tasked with improving customer service. This team has seven members, all of whom have worked in the store at least five years. Makayla is aware that two of the members on this team, Annika and Alex, have a history of making subtle personal attacks against one another and undermining each other's work. This behavior went unchecked because the prior assistant manager avoided dealing with the conflict.

If Makayla came to you asking your advice about leading this team and managing the conflict:

- What would you suggest she do to help her understand the team dynamic better?

- What questions could she ask? And to whom?
- What actions would you encourage her to take? Or not take?
- How would you help her discern what to do regarding the relational conflict between Alex and Annika?
- How might she begin to help shift the team's overall focus toward productive task conflict aimed at improving customer service?

References

Alvarez, Cecilio. 2017. "Controversy with Civility." In *Leadership for a Better World: Understanding the Social Change Model of Leadership Development*. Edited by Susan Komives and Wendy Wagner, 2nd ed., 149–70. San Francisco: Jossey-Bass.

Barrett, Richard. 2017. *The Values-Driven Organization*. 2nd ed. New York: Routledge.

Blake, Robert, and Jane Mouton. 1964. *The Managerial Grid*. Houston: Gulf Publishing.

Bohm, David. 1996. *On Dialogue*. Edited by Lee Nicol. New York: Routledge.

Bolman, Lee G., and Terrence E. Deal. 2017. *Reframing Organizations: Artistry, Choice, and Leadership*. 6th ed. Hoboken: Wiley.

Bradley, Bret, Bennett Postlethwaite, Anthony Klotz, Maria Hamdani, and Kenneth Brown. 2012. "Reaping the Benefits of Task Conflict in Teams: The Critical Role of Team Psychological Safety Climate." *Journal of Applied Psychology* 97 (1): 151–58. https://doi.org/10.1037/a0024200

Colwill, Deborah A. 2005. "Dialogical Learning and a Renewed Epistemology: Analysis of Cultural and Educational Shifts from Modernity toward Postmodernity." PhD diss., Trinity International University.

DeRue, D. Scott, and Kristina Workman. 2013. "Toward a Positive and Dynamic Theory of Leadership Development." In *The Oxford Handbook of Positive Organizational Scholarship*. Edited by Kim S. Cameron and Gretchen M. Spreitzer, 784–97. New York: Oxford University Press.

Edmondson, Amy C. 2019. *The Fearless Organization: Creating Psychological Safety in the Workplace for Learning, Innovation, and Growth*. Hoboken: Wiley.

Edmondson, Amy C., and Diana McLain Smith. 2006. "Too Hot to Handle? How to Manage Relationship Conflict." *California Management Review* 49 (1): 6–31.

Elmer, Duane. 1993. *Cross-Cultural Conflict: Building Relationships for Effective Ministry*. Downers Grove: IVP Academic.

Fisher, Roger, William L. Ury, and Bruce Patton. 2011. *Getting to Yes: Negotiating Agreement Without Giving In*. 3rd ed. London: Penguin Books.

Follett, Mary Parker. [1925] 2013. *Dynamic Administration: The Collected Papers of Mary Parker Follett*. Illustrated ed. Mansfield Centre: Martino Fine Books.

Hofstede, Geert. 1993. "Cultural Constraints in Management Theories." *Academy of Management Executive* 7 (1): 81–94.

House, Robert J., Peter W. Dorfman, Mansour Javidan, Paul J. Hanges, and Mary Sully de Luque. 2014. *Strategic Leadership Across Cultures: GLOBE Study of CEO Leadership Behavior and Effectiveness in 24 Countries*. Thousand Oaks: SAGE Publications.

House, Robert J., Paul J. Hanges, Mansour Javidan, Peter W. Dorfman, and Vipin Gupta, eds. 2004. *Culture, Leadership, and Organizations: The GLOBE Study of 62 Societies*. Thousand Oaks: SAGE Publications.

Isaacs, William. 1993. "Taking Flight: Dialogue, Collective Thinking, and Organizational Learning." *Organizational Dynamics* 22 (2): 24–39. https://doi.org/10.1016/0090-2616(93)90051-2

———. 1999. *Dialogue: The Art of Thinking Together*. New York: Currency.

Javidan, Mansour, Peter W. Dorfman, Mary Sully de Luque, and Robert J. House. 2006. "In the Eye of the Beholder: Cross Cultural Lessons in Leadership from Project GLOBE." *The Academy of Management Perspectives* 20 (1): 67–90. https://doi.org/10.5465/AMP.2006.19873410

Kilmann, Ralph H., and Kenneth W. Thomas. 1977. "Developing a Forced-Choice Measure of Conflict-Handling Behavior: The 'Mode' Instrument." *Educational and Psychological Measurement* 37 (2): 309–25. https://doi.org/10.1177/001316447703700204

Kouzes, James M., and Barry Z. Posner. 2017. *The Leadership Challenge: How to Make Extraordinary Things Happen in Organizations*. 6th ed. Hoboken: Wiley.

Liddle, David. 2017. *Managing Conflict: A Practical Guide to Resolution in the Workplace*. New York: Kogan Page.

Palmer, Donald C. 2020. *Managing Conflict Creatively*. 30th Anniversary ed. Littleton: William Carey Publishing.

Pondy, Louis R. 1967. "Organizational Conflict: Concepts and Models." *Administrative Science Quarterly* 12 (2): 296–320. https://doi.org/10.2307/2391553

Rahim, M. Afzalur. 2015. *Managing Conflict in Organizations*. 4th ed. New Brunswick: Routledge.

Raines, Susan S. 2020. *Conflict Management for Managers: Resolving Workplace, Client, and Policy Disputes*. 2nd ed. Lanham: Rowman and Littlefield Publishers.

Riggio, Ronald E., and Rebecca J. Reichard. 2008. "The Emotional and Social Intelligences of Effective Leadership: An Emotional and Social Skill Approach." *Journal of Managerial Psychology* 23 (2): 169–85. https://doi.org/10.1108/02683940810850808

Schein, Edgar H., and Peter A. Schein. 2018. *Humble Leadership: The Power of Relationships, Openness, and Trust*. Oakland: Berrett-Koehler Publishers.

Trompenaars, Fons, and Charles Hampden-Turner. 2012. *Riding the Waves of Culture: Understanding Diversity in Global Business*. 3rd ed. New York: McGraw-Hill Education.

Zhao, Emma Y., Sherry M. B. Thatcher, and Karen A. Jehn. 2019. "Instigating, Engaging in, and Managing Group Conflict: A Review of the Literature Addressing the Critical Role of the Leader in Group Conflict." *Academy of Management Annals* 13 (1): 112–47. https://doi.org/10.5465/annals.2016.0153

4 Power

Introduction

What do you think when you hear the word *power*? Some might say power is exercising strength, like a powerful athlete lifting heavy weights. Or power is expressing creativity, like a powerful jazz performance. Power is generating energy, like the abundant flow of electricity from a power plant. The word "power" derives from the Latin verb *potere*; "the central meaning of *potere* is to be able. Power is the ability to affect something or to be affected by something" (Silber 1979, 191). Thus, power can denote the ability to exercise strength, express creativity, or generate energy.

What about the use of power in organizations? Is gaining power an end in itself, or is it a means to an end? Is power a negative, positive, or neutral phenomenon? Authors debate these and other questions. They also describe power in various ways: bases of power, sources of power, types of power, and faces of power. These varied and overlapping ways of interpreting the concept of power can be confusing. Given the variation, it is worthwhile to interact with some key ideas from the literature and build our own understanding of power in organizations from the balcony, the road, and with regard to organizational moorings. The main idea that will track through the chapter is that the essence of power is "to be able."

Views From the Balcony

Keep in mind, the benefit of the balcony view is that it gives a broader vantage point. As such, the balcony view on power will describe some prominent concepts for reflective consideration.

DOI: 10.4324/9780429323959-4

Early Writings on Power in Organizations

Many would agree that power can be used for good or for evil. Yet, Crouch (2013, 10) notes, "Underlying much of the academic fascination with power . . . is the presupposition that power is essentially about coercion." If the central meaning of power is "to be able," where does this presupposition about power as coercion come from? Looking at how early organization theorists conceptualized power gives us some insight.

Early writings on the use of power in organizations emerged following the Second World War (Clegg, Courpasson, and Phillips 2011). Building on the mechanistic framework of "Scientific Management" (Taylor 1911), the priority was efficiency and effectiveness in which management directed workers' behavior resulting in predictable outputs. Properly applying the science of engineering to management "would not only legitimate the manager as a new class of highly skilled employee but also justify the entire structures of control in which they were inserted. It would make these structures authoritative" (Clegg, Courpasson, and Phillips 2011, 97). Thus, authority was derived from organizational structure, whereas power was covertly used to gain compliance.

Consequently, some early writers describe power as coercive in nature. To illustrate, two seminal definitions are offered. Power "is the probability that one actor within a social relationship will be in a position to carry out his own will despite resistance, regardless of the basis on which this probability rests" (Weber [1947] 2012, 152). Another oft-quoted definition, "*A has power over B to the extent that he can get B to do something that B would not otherwise do*" (Dahl 1957, 202–203). Three aspects of power arise from early definitions. First, power is a relation between or among people. Second, power involves mutual dependence in that "each party is in a position, to some degree, to grant or deny, facilitate or hinder, the other's gratification . . . In short, *power resides implicitly in the other's dependency*" (Emerson 1962, 32). A third aspect of power is the deliberate use of sanctions which "can consist of manipulations of rewards, punishments, or both" (Bacharach and Lawler 1980, 24). In summary, early definitions highlight three aspects of power: relational, dependence, and sanctioning (ibid., 15).

If the central meaning of power is "to be able," then early theorists saw power as the ability of one person or group to assert their will over another person or group despite resistance. In the next section, power-over will be explored alongside of other modes of power.

Power-Over, Power-With, and Other Modes of Power

A "mode" is a way or manner in which something occurs or is experienced, expressed, or done. This section will explore four modes of power: power-over, power-to, power-from, and power-with.

As stated earlier, early theorists viewed power as the ability to covertly control workers' behavior despite their resistance in order to achieve preferred outcomes. This power mode is known as "power-over" and is "coercive" in nature (Follett [1925] 2013, 101). Hollander and Offermann (1990, 179) observe "power-over" is "explicit or implicit dominance." Parsons (1963b, 232) notes power is plagued by the "zero-sum problem." Zero-sum refers to a situation in which the gain of one actor implies the loss for another. For example, acquiring and hoarding resources with the intent of making others dependent for the resources is a power-over tactic based on a zero-sum mindset. Competition to control the system "acts in a Darwinian way" (Mintzberg 1983, 226). Power-over is used to enhance one's own survival (Pfeffer 2013).

Power-to is a second mode of power. Hollander and Offermann (1990, 179) note that unlike power-over, "power-to" mode "gives individuals the opportunity to act more freely within some realms of organizational operations, through power sharing, or what is commonly called *empowerment*." The notion of power-to stems from Talcott Parsons (Clegg, Courpasson, and Phillips 2011). Parsons' view of power "is not to punish but to secure performance" in the interest of "effective collective action (goal attainment)" (1963a, 45). Consequently, power is not merely controlling power-over, but can be empowering power-to, which creatively accomplishes goals and changes the nature of coworker relations. Yet, Habermas (1987, 271) argues that while this type of interaction may be "in the interest of both parties, a person taking orders is structurally disadvantaged in relation to a person with the power to give them." Power-to mode might empower employees more than power-over mode; but, power differentials still exist within power-to mode. Alongside this concept, "there remains a pervasive belief that to empower others is to lose power oneself. In short although power is not a zero-sum quality, it is often perceived as such" (Hollander and Offermann 1990, 184). Lastly, "Power itself isn't 'over' or 'to' in a transcendent way; it is 'over' or 'to' depending on the specific situation and the contingent position of the agents involved in the relation" (Clegg, Courpasson, and Phillips 2011, 191).

A third mode of power is "power-from" which is "the ability to resist the power of others by effectively fending off their unwanted demands" (Hollander and Offermann 1990, 179). When faced with unwanted demands from a boss or coworker, power-from wisdom has the potential to help in terms of keeping a cool head, reading the situation, determining how to act or not act, and knowing when to ask for outside help. Fairholm (2009, 68) observes, "People use power defensively to prevent someone from doing something we don't like or that will hurt us." Power-from can be expressed in many ways; simply put, power-from is the ability "to handle an undesirable influence attempt initiated by someone else" (Yukl 2013, 209).

Power-with is a fourth mode of power. The concept of "power-with" was first articulated by Follett (1924). In her view, power was an inevitable part of life, but not necessarily autocratic in nature. Follett ([1925] 2013, 101) states, "whereas power usually means power-over, the power of some person or group over some other person or group, it is possible to develop the conception of power-with, a jointly developed power, a coactive, not a coercive power." VeneKlasen and Miller (2007, 45) agree that power-with is about "finding common ground among different interests and building collective strength. Based on mutual support, solidarity, and collaboration, power-with multiplies individual talents and knowledge. Power-with can help build bridges across different interests to transform or reduce social conflict and promote equitable relations."

In summary, if the essence of power is "to be able," then power-over is the ability to overtly direct and control the work of others; power-to is the ability to guide and empower others to do their work; power-from is the ability to resist unwanted power demands; and power-with is the ability to collaboratively build power and work together. We will refer to these modes of power throughout the chapter to help us navigate through the dense forest of the use of power in organizations.

Pinning Down Power?

Since power is a complex concept, it has been suggested that rather than pinning it down with a precise definition, perhaps a broad definition is needed instead (Bacharach and Lawler 1980; Hardy 1985). To that end, Hardy (1985, 385) offers a definition of power as "the ability to affect the behavior of others in a conscious and deliberate way." Mintzberg (1983, 4) defines power "as the capacity to effect (or affect) organizational outcomes." Both definitions agree that the essence of power is "to be able." One view focuses on affecting behavior; the other focuses on outcomes. Both move away from the early formulaic definitions of "agent A over target B despite B's resistance." However, both retain a view of power as deliberately exercising influence or control. Another broad definition of power is "the potential ability to influence behavior, to change the course of events, to overcome resistance, and to get people to do things that they would not otherwise do" (Pfeffer 1992, 30). This definition echoes the power-over theorists and clearly carries the sanctioning aspect of power.

Even more recently, a literature review by Sturm and Antonakis (2015, 139) reports three essential characteristics of power from previous definitions: "Power is about having (a) *discretion* (agency) to act and (b) the *means* (innate, position) to (c) *enforce* one's will. That is, a powerful agent is one who can exogenously affect his or her environment or others at will." Whether defining power broadly or attempting to pin it down specifically, the early ideas about power continue to inform and shape our views of power in organizations today.

Assumptions, Motivation, and the Two Faces of Power

Managers use power to accomplish goals. But, what influences the manager's choice of power mode and practice? We will briefly look at two possible responses to this question: (1) assumptions that managers carry about employees and (2) motivation and the two faces of power.

Management Assumptions

McGregor ([1960] 2006, 45) argued, "Behind every managerial decision or action are assumptions about human nature and behavior." McGregor described two sets of assumptions about human beings that inform the practice of management: Theory X and Theory Y.

Theory X holds three assumptions about human beings: "The average person dislikes work and will avoid it if possible"; "People need to be directed and controlled"; and "People want security, not responsibility" (Northouse 2021, 58). Regarding Theory X, McGregor ([1960] 2006, 181) states, "Since an underlying assumption is that people must be made to do what is necessary for the success of the enterprise, attention is naturally directed to the techniques of direction and control." The assumptions of Theory X align with management theorists such as Taylor (1911) and the use of abovementioned power-over mode.

Theory Y assumes: "The average person does not inherently dislike work. Doing work is as natural as play"; "People will show responsibility and self-control toward goals to which they are committed"; and "In the proper environment, the average person learns to accept and seek responsibility" (Northouse 2021, 59–60). Management's role is not to coerce and control employees but to create opportunities where both the employees and the organization thrive. The central Theory Y principle is "integration: the creation of conditions such that the members of the organization can achieve their own goals *best* by directing their efforts toward the success of the enterprise" (McGregor [1960] 2006, 67–68). Integration "requires active and responsible participation" by each individual in decisions affecting their own careers (ibid., 137). Note the similarity with the empowerment of power-to mode and the integrative nature of power-with mode described earlier.

According to McGregor, most managers have a blend of Theory X and Y assumptions about people; therefore, his aim was to raise awareness of these assumptions that directly impact management practice. McGregor's call to critical reflection is a timeless practice that is as relevant today as it was in his day.

Motivation and the Two Faces of Power

What motives undergird management behavior? Carl, Gupta, and Javidan (2004, 515) report, "managers are motivated by three basic and *nonconscious* needs—the need for achievement, the need for affiliation, and the need for power." Their statement is based on the research of McClelland and Burnham ([1976] 2003), in which three "motivational groups" of managers were identified: "achievement," "affiliative," and "institutional."

Achievement managers "focus on setting goals and reaching them, but they put their own achievement and recognition first," and they are also called "personal-power managers" (ibid., 117; 121). Affiliative managers "need to be liked more than they need to get things done" (117). Institutional managers focus on the use of power and the influence it affords. Their power motivation is "the desire to have impact, to be strong and influential" (119).

Regarding the power motivation of achievement and institutional managers, McClelland (1970, 29) draws the distinction between personalized and socialized power which are the "two faces of power." First, "The negative or personal face of power is characterized by the dominance submission mode: if I win, you lose" (ibid., 41). The leader treats other people as "pawns" to accomplish their own goals (41). Second, "The positive or socialized face of power is characterized by a concern for group goals" (41). The leader helps the group to find inspiring goals, formulate the goals, locate resources needed, and encourages group members' confidence and competence to achieve their goals (41). Power motivation must be tempered by maturity and self-control in order to foster a positive work climate (McClelland and Burnham [1976] 2003, 117). Institutional managers motivated by the socialized face of power are more effective than achievement or affiliative managers, and "their direct reports have a greater sense of responsibility, see organizational goals more clearly, and exhibit more team spirit" (ibid., 117). In summary, effective managers are not merely motivated by the need for personal achievement, or the need to be liked by coworkers, but rather by a desire to inspire people to work together to achieve their shared goals.

The balcony perspective allows us to pull back and view the big picture. Reflecting on our own assumptions and motivations in the use of power in organizations is important because the use of power will inevitably display itself in our actions, particularly when we are under pressure.

Cultural Power Dynamics

Cultural values permeate management practices including the use of power. Moreover, "acceptable management practices found in one country are hardly guaranteed to work in a different country" (Javidan et al. 2006, 70).

Daniels and Greguras (2014, 1203) observe, "One cultural value, power distance, is especially important in organizational research because power is fundamental to all relationships, is inherent in hierarchical organizations, and affects many organizational processes and outcomes." House and Javidan (2004, 12) define power distance as "the degree to which members of an organization or society expect and agree that power should be stratified and concentrated at higher levels of an organization or government."

High power distance "reflects unequal power distribution in a society. Countries that scored high on this cultural practice are more stratified economically, socially, and politically; those in positions of authority expect, and receive, obedience" (Javidan et al. 2006, 70). Conversely, low power distance denotes a "limited dependence of subordinates on bosses, and there is a preference for consultation (that is, *interdependence* between boss and subordinate)" (Hofstede and Hofstede 2005, 45). In low power distance cultures, "the distaste for large power differentials is often based on the beliefs that power corrupts, and that excessive power results in the abuse of power, from which people in less powerful positions have no recourse" (Carl, Gupta, and Javidan 2004, 518).

Sharing power is "expected to facilitate entrepreneurial innovation, to allow broader participation in education, and to constrain the abuse of power and corruption" (ibid., 559). Although power differentials exist in hierarchical structures, "substantial gains can be obtained by reducing the level of power distance within an organization. Reduced power distance can contribute to the flexibility of the organization and enhance competence building and learning" (534). And yet, in high power distance cultures, "it may be more difficult to initiate and sustain egalitarian power practices" when organizational members "have been accustomed to depend on their supervisors for direction and decision making" (534). In addition, high power distance "preempts the society from questioning, learning, and adapting as there is little opportunity for debate and voicing of divergent views. Asking questions may be interpreted or regarded as criticizing and blaming, and therefore may be prohibited" (559).

Life Along the Road

Our focus now shifts to the organizational road, although much of the conceptual work from the balcony will carry over here. The on-the-ground aspects we will explore include the social bases of power, the use of position and personal power, as well as some common tactics and practices of power.

Social Bases of Power

A well-known typology by French and Raven (1959) sought to identify "the social bases of power." A "base" is a point from which something can develop or be built upon. The bases of power are what individuals control that enable them to bring about their intended outcomes. French and Raven (1959, 150) suggest power involves "a dyadic relation" between the person who exerts power and the recipient of this behavior. From the many possible bases of power, they narrowed the field to five: reward power, coercive power, legitimate power, referent power, and expert power (ibid., 155). Subsequently, Raven (1965) added informational power as a sixth base.

With regard to their earlier work, Raven (2008, 1) states "we first defined social influence as a change in the belief, attitude, or behavior of a person (the target of influence), which results from the action of another person (an influencing agent)." Like the theorists of their day, French and Raven's understanding of power emphasized the relational, dependence, and sanctioning aspects of power mentioned previously. These three aspects are visible in the brief descriptions of the six power bases provided in the following text.

Reward power is simply "the ability to reward" (French and Raven 1959, 156). The main idea is that rewards are used by the influencing agent to gain compliance of the target. Essential to reward power is the target's perception that the agent not only has the desired resources, but also has the ability and willingness to mediate these rewards. Examples of reward incentives include "pay raises, promotions or special work privileges" (Raven 2008, 2).

Coercive power is "the ability to mediate punishments" (French and Raven 1959, 156). More specifically, coercion is used to gain compliance through inflicting penalties, but also through removing or decreasing things the target actually desires. Coercion rests "on the ability to constrain, block, interfere, or punish" (Bolman and Deal 2017, 192). Coercive power gains strength as a result of the target's heightened expectation of being punished "if he fails to conform to the influence attempt" (French and Raven 1959, 157). Examples of negative consequences include "demotion, termination, or undesirable work assignments" (Raven 2008, 2).

Similarities between reward power and coercive power have been observed. Both types of power are strengthened when the target believes the agent will deliver rewards or punishment as a consequence of the target's behavior. Effective reward power will tend to increase attraction and lower resistance of the target toward the agent, whereas coercive power will decrease attraction and fuel resistance (French and Raven 1959). Both reward and coercive power differ from other bases of power in that "their effectiveness requires surveillance by the influencing agent" (Raven 2008, 2).

Legitimate power rises from the target's perception that the agent "has a legitimate right to prescribe behavior for him" (French and Raven 1959, 156). This type of power is "based on norms and expectations regarding behaviors that are appropriate in a given role or position" (Bass and Bass 2008, 282).

Referent power "refers to a subordinate's feeling of oneness with the leader and a desire to identify with, emulate, and internalize the values of a superior" (Carl, Gupta, and Javidan 2004, 514). If the target is "highly attracted" to the agent, then the target will desire to maintain a close relationship with the agent (French and Raven 1959, 161). As attraction and identification grow, then the agent's referent power over the target increases. Bass and Bass (2008, 274) suggest "Liked, respected, and esteemed leaders have referent power."

Expert power relies on the target's assessment of the influence agent's expertise, "in relation to his own knowledge as well as against an absolute standard" (French and Raven 1959, 163). Expert knowledge and skill only remain a source of power as long as the need for the expertise continues. Therefore, "Expert power is more fluid than fixed in a position or person" (Bass and Bass 2008, 274).

Raven (1992, 221) states, "Information power, or persuasion, is based on the information, or logical argument, that the influencing agent can present to the target in order to implement change." Additionally, it "involves both the access to vital information and control over its distribution to others" (Yukl 2013, 192).

The social bases of power emphasize interactions between the influencing agent and the target of influence. French and Raven's work "pointed out that individuals in organizations do not just derive their power from their positions of authority, but other sources too" (Fleming and Spicer 2014, 250). Mendenhall et al. (2018, 8) state while the "bases of power seem straightforward, it turns out that the enactment of power between leaders and subordinates is complex and sometimes counterintuitive." Furthermore, "power is not a unidirectional, top-down force that flows from manager to subordinate" (ibid., 8). French and Raven (1959, 150) acknowledge, "The processes of power are pervasive, complex, and often disguised in our society." Lastly, two overarching categories encompass French and Raven's work: position power and personal power. Position power includes reward, coercive, legitimate, and information power which are organizationally derived, whereas personal power includes referent and expert power which are individually derived (Student 1968; Yukl 2013).

Position Power

Position power is organizationally derived through the person's role in the hierarchy (Student 1968). Bass and Bass (2008, 268) argue, "individuals who are in positions of power not only can assert it successfully, but also can maintain and increase their level of power. Thus power-oriented individuals who gain positions of power will strive to retain and increase their power, since they are in a favored position to ensure that their power continues." Many possible expressions of position power exist. To illustrate, two examples will be explored in the following sections: embedding power in organizational design and structure and leveraging power from one's organizational role.

Embedding Position Power

While position power is clearly seen in overt control or ownership of an organization, power is also embedded in the design and structure of an organizational system (Fleming and Spicer 2014). Depending on the kinds of influence and control, some actors have more opportunity than others to exhibit power. For example, Mintzberg (1984, 209) describes five "internal coalition" forms of power: "*personalized* (the personal controls of a leader dominate, such as the issuing of ad hoc orders); *bureaucratic* (formal standards dominate); *ideologic* (the norms of a strong internal ideology dominate); *professional* (the technical skills and knowledge of experts dominate); and *politicized* (political or conflictive forces dominate)." The organizational design, structure, and culture create various advantages or disadvantages in exercising power. Two illustrations of embedded position power are favoring the influential and selecting corporate goals.

Organizational systems favor influential members. Some organizations "give high power members obvious markers of their privileged status, such as ostentatious corner offices, top-of-the-line technology, company cars, and special parking spaces. Such explicit cues make the power differences between individuals obvious" (Caza, Tiedens, and Lee 2011, 15). However, organizations vary in how power differences are expressed. Even when overt power cues are downplayed, differences in power are "conveyed through implicit cues such as verbal and nonverbal signals of deference or dominance" (ibid., 15). Although overt power markers are downplayed, embedded position power dynamics favoring the influential are still at work.

Wide-reaching position power is afforded to leaders who name and inculcate the organizational values which directly impact the selection and implementation of specific corporate goals. Bolman and Deal (2017, 193) state, "Elites and opinion leaders often have substantial ability to shape meaning and articulate myths that express identity, beliefs, and values. Viewed positively, this fosters meaning and hope. Viewed cynically, elites can convince others to accept and support things not in their best interests." Habermas (1987, 271) adds, "the person in power uses his definitional power to establish which goals are going to count as collective ones" and this engenders a "structural disadvantage" for some members.

Leveraging Position Power

Position power can also be leveraged from one's organizational role. Two examples are prime location in the hierarchy and the skillful use of resources.

Prime location in the hierarchy affords at least two power advantages: the agency of formal authority and a strategic position from which to act. Formal authority means that "power resides in the position, not the incumbent" (Brass and Burkhardt 1993, 444). This functional oversight of others provides the agency of "legitimate power" (French and Raven 1959). Prime location also offers a strategic position from which to act. Being "central in the workflow and communication structure" allows one "to develop and exercise influence" (Pfeffer 1997, 145). Likewise, a strategic location "gives the individual access to information and control over access to people" (Anderson and Brion 2014, 75). Pettigrew (1972, 190) adds, "Gatekeepers, those who sit at the junction of a number of communication channels, are in a position to regulate the flow of demands and potentially control decisional outcomes" with perhaps a "self-interested filtering of information during a decision process."

Skillful use and control of resources is another means of position power (Pettigrew 1972). Anderson and Brion (2014, 69) highlight the advantage of "asymmetric control over valued resources." Asymmetric control imposes a power-over dependence since "power accrues to people who control resources that others cannot access" (Pfeffer 2010, 104). Some argue power increases by attaining scarce critical resources; however, Clegg (1989, 98) observes "almost any phenomenon can be a resource in the appropriate context. The trick resides in constructing the context in which those resources one seeks to employ acquire a privileged status."

Personal Power

Personal power is individually derived through the capacity of the actors themselves (Student 1968). In other words, personal power arises from the characteristics, relationships, and behavior of the individual. Two types of personal power are described in the following sections: building interpersonal influence and utilizing valuable knowledge.

Building Interpersonal Influence

Agents use interpersonal influence as a means to relationally persuade other organizational members toward a goal or purpose. Two examples are coalitions and social networks.

Coalitions are alliances of people who come together for a common mission. In organizations, coalitions apply pressure on individuals or groups to gain support for a proposed change or a new initiative (Kipnis, Schmidt, and Wilkinson 1980). Forming coalitions also involves allying with persons outside the organization for mutual support (Fairholm 2009). Pfeffer (1992, 104) notes, "One of the ways in which we can build alliances and coalitions is by helping people with whom we have ties to obtain positions of power."

The building and maintenance of social networks is another form of interpersonal influence. Social networks are the ties among actors that represent the presence of some type of relationship or absence of a relationship (Brass and Krackhardt 2012). In organizational life, social networking aims at "building, maintaining, and using informal relationships that possess the (potential) benefit of facilitating work-related activities" (Wolff and Moser 2009, 196). Moreover, closely observing the relational patterns in an organization affords advantages. For example, attentiveness to social networks may uncover "structural holes" which are "gaps in the social world across which there are no current connections" (Kilduff and Tsai 2003, 28). Upon identification of structural holes, one might seek "to increase their social capital by performing the liaison role of connecting two otherwise disconnected cliques, or by bridging from one group to which they belong to another group that they join" (ibid., 28).

Utilizing Valuable Knowledge

A second way to express personal power is through utilizing valuable knowledge. Two examples include knowledge of organizational power dynamics and the effective use of expert knowledge.

Astuteness regarding the use of power in organizations is necessary to grow personal power. Deepening one's knowledge about power dynamics includes a general awareness about the use of power in organizations, attentiveness to specific power dynamics unique to an organization, and carefully observing the personal power and social networking behaviors of others. Growing in knowledge about power dynamics in general as well as specific contextual use of power is key to getting things done in organizations.

Personal power is enhanced through utilizing expert knowledge. Bass and Bass (2008, 273) observe that "Expert power may be manifest in information, knowledge, and wisdom: in good decisions; in sound judgment; and in accurate perceptions of reality." Expert power "is bestowed on those who find a critical function in which to practice their irreplaceable expertise" and "only those who provide an expertise difficult to replace gain power" (Mintzberg 1983, 170; 167). However, "Power is lost because changed circumstances render previous skills or networks obsolete" (Pfeffer 1992, 307). Therefore, keeping current in expert or technical knowledge is necessary to retain expert power.

Position power and personal power greatly overlap in actual use. Yukl (2013, 216) observes, "Effective leaders rely more on personal power than on position power and they use power in a subtle, careful fashion that minimizes status differentials and avoids threats to the target person's self-esteem. To contrast, leaders who exercise power in an arrogant, manipulative, domineering manner are likely to engender resentment and resistance."

Tactics and Practices of Power

Traveling the organizational road also includes the tactics and practices of power, that is, the skillful use of specific strategic behaviors to bring about a particular end. The power behaviors described in the following sections instinctively align according to power-over and power-with modes. Power-over tactics are generally thought to be "coercive," whereas power-with practices are "coactive" (Follett 1924). And yet, the motive, relationships, context, and intended outcomes greatly matter in the use of power behaviors. For example, power-over tactics could be used in an emergency to assertively direct the efforts of coworkers to get the situation under control for the good of all concerned. In this case, a temporary use of power-over tactics may be warranted. Alternatively, a leader could manipulatively use power-with practices to steal collaborative team efforts and claim sole credit for the work. This self-promoting behavior runs counter to power-with ethos since it violates the good of others.

Power is a relational and contextual matter. What constitutes power tactics or practices in one organization, context, or culture may not apply to the same degree in another. Discernment should be exercised regarding how to engage in a particular local context. Moreover, these on-the-road behaviors might be used for the good of all concerned; for self-advancing purposes; or perhaps a tacit blend of both. Power-over tactics and power-with practices will be briefly discussed in subsequent sections.

Power-over Tactics

Theory X assumptions lead "to an emphasis on the tactics of control—to procedures and techniques for telling people what to do, for determining whether they are doing it, and for administering rewards and punishments" (McGregor [1960] 2006, 181). While power-over mode seems to be "inevitable in organizational life, it always carries with it the specter of abuse" (Hollander and Offermann 1990, 187). As a result, it is best to avoid using coercive tactics because they are "difficult to use and likely to result in undesirable side effects. Coercion often arouses anger or resentment, and it may result in retaliation" (Yukl 2013, 199).

With these cautionary statements in mind, several power-over tactics are briefly described in the following paragraphs. The rationale for including them here is not to endorse their use, but to expose their use so that we might be more prepared to deal with them on the organizational road. Some common power-over tactics are legitimizing, pressuring, surveillance, ingratiation, manipulation, intimidation, subversion, and exchange.

Legitimizing tactics are based in the formal authority and traditions of the organization (Fairholm 2009). A manager declares a legitimate right to act, based on their organizational role or position. For example, a manager might assert "the legitimacy of a request by claiming the authority or right to make it or by verifying that it is consistent with organizational policies, rules, practices, or traditions" (Yukl and Tracey 1992, 526).

Pressuring is a power-over tactic which involves "demands, threats, frequent checking, or persistent reminders to influence the target to carry out a request" (Yukl 2013, 202). Agents are not likely to use pressure tactics with their bosses but more likely to use them with subordinates (Yukl and Tracey 1992).

A third tactic is surveillance. As noted earlier, both coercive and reward power use surveillance to monitor compliance of the target (Raven 2008). Surveillance may take the form of "supervision, routinization, formulation, mechanization and legislations which seek to effect increasing control of employees' behavior, dispositions and embodiment, precisely because they are organization members" (Clegg 1989, 100).

Ingratiation includes "praising, politely asking, acting humble, making the other person feel important, and acting friendly" (Brass and Burkhardt 1993, 447). The agent "uses praise and flattery before or during an influence attempt" (Yukl 2013, 202). While ingratiation may have a positive facade, it is included with power-over tactics because it deliberately attempts to win the favor of another primarily for one's own benefit.

Manipulation has many covert expressions. The aim is to deceptively handle or control others in an unfair or unethical manner. Fairholm (2009, 19) asserts, "The key to manipulation is masking intent to affect the other person's behavior directly. Manipulation does not evoke a counter reaction from the target, since our targets do not know that they are targets of our power use." For example, a meeting agenda may be manipulated "through carefully managing what is on the table for debate and who is able to participate in the debate" (Fleming and Spicer 2014, 254). These dynamics "exclude and devalue the concerns and representation of other less powerful groups" (VeneKlasen and Miller 2007, 47).

Intimidation is a power-over tactic that raises coercion to a caustic level. This tactic inflicts fear by threatening punishment if the target fails to conform to the influence attempt (Raven 2008). The agent's goal is to persuade the target that the agent is "ready and willing to pay the costs that coercion implies" in order to get the target to do what the agent wants (Raven 2008, 6).

Subversion is the intentional undermining of power or authority of a leader, group, or system. As a power-over behavior, it seeks to disrupt the agenda of a competitor. For example, "blocking" is a form of subversion that "attempts to stop the target person from carrying out some action" through "engaging in a work slowdown" or "threatening to stop working with the target person" (Kipnis, Schmidt, and Wilkinson 1980, 447). Another example is "minimizing the target" in which the agent uses "subtle 'put-downs' which decrease the target's self-esteem, or confidence" thereby increasing the agent's expert or legitimate power in the eyes of others (Raven 1992, 224).

The eighth tactic is exchange of favors which could be a power-over tactic or power-with practice depending on the context and whether or not the exchange benefits only the agent, or if indeed, mutual benefit is accomplished. Pfeffer (2010, 97) states, "Helping people out in almost any fashion engages the norm of reciprocity—the powerful, almost universal behavioral principle that favors must be repaid." The agent provides "information, money, materials, psychological support, friendship, or other needs to the target, and then uses the sense of obligation incurred to later induce compliance" (Fairholm 2009, 109).

Power-over tactics attempt to control or modify the behavior of another person or group, despite their resistance. This type of behavior raises justifiable concerns about possible exploitation of human beings (Hicks 2018). Is there another way to exercise power? We will look at power-with practices next.

Power-with Practices

Theory Y assumptions about people underlie power-with practices. Managers who hold these assumptions seek to intentionally create integrative conditions where both the organization and its members thrive (McGregor [1960] 2006). Likewise, encouraging collaborative responsibility to exercise coactive power will grow the mindset and practices of power-with (Follett 1924). The role of leaders is to increase the coactive power capacity across the organization. Leaders need to coach the organizational community in collaborative power-with practices which are experientially learned. Growing coactive power takes time, education, and training to develop. However, if "interactive influence" is routinely practiced, then "power-with may be built up" (Follett [1925] 2013, 105). According to Follett (1924, xiii), the use of power in organizations is inevitable; and, the best use of power is "power-with." To illustrate, a few power-with practices are described as follows: rational persuasion, inspirational appeal, strong reputation, and consultation.

Rational persuasion uses logical arguments and factual evidence to persuade coworkers that a proposal or request is worthwhile and workable (Kipnis, Schmidt, and Wilkinson. 1980). This practice is strengthened when practiced in community. Proposals will be stronger if coworkers critically engage about the substance. Generative dialogue will help the group grow in coactive power. However, if an individual or group using rational persuasion deliberately conceals important information or misrepresents their coworkers, then rational persuasion deteriorates into manipulation or subversion.

Inspirational appeal aims at "the values, ideals, and aspirations" of coworkers to "arouse enthusiasm" and gain commitment for a request or proposal (Yukl and Tracey 1992, 526). This practice is effectively used with subordinates (ibid., 525). Theory Y assumes "people will exercise self-direction and self-control in the achievement of organizational objectives *to the degree that they are committed to those objectives*" (McGregor [1960] 2006, 76). Therefore, appealing to genuinely "shared aspirations" is essential (Kouzes and Posner 2017, 15). However, if inspirational appeals are manipulatively used to push coworkers into complying with something that is not in their best interest, then these appeals have deteriorated into coercion. Again, collaborative integration grows when the goals of both the employees and the organization are mutually addressed.

A strong reputation "builds on expertise. In almost any field, people develop records of accomplishment based on their prior performance. Opportunities and influence flow to people with strong reputations" (Bolman and Deal 2017, 192). Likewise, a statement "will carry more 'weight' if made by someone with a high reputation for competence, for reliability, for good judgment" (Parsons 1963a, 50). A strong reputation provides a power-with opportunity to be a trusted ally to coworkers who would benefit from inclusion, support, encouragement, or protection.

Consultation happens when a coworker "seeks your participation in planning a strategy, activity, or change for which your support and assistance are desired" and ideally, they would "modify a proposal to deal with your concerns and suggestions" (Yukl and Tracey 1992, 526). Consultation can easily become ingratiation, if merely used to manipulate. For consultation to be mutually beneficial, a good working relationship based on trust between actors is essential.

Power-with behaviors have the potential of engaging individuals in the collective work of an organization through coactive responsibility. And yet, "In reality, power is both dynamic and multidimensional, changing according to context, circumstance and interest. Its expressions and forms can range from domination and resistance to collaboration and transformation" (VeneKlasen and Miller 2007, 39).

Focus on Organizational Moorings

Metaphorically speaking, organizational moorings provide guidance for how we conduct ourselves especially during stormy unstable times. After a brief introduction, we will look at two examples of moorings that could guide the use of power in organizations.

Using power for good can be life-giving. Crouch (2013, 10) observes, "the deepest form of power is creation." When people collaboratively create things together, they learn, grow, and stretch. For instance, the work of a creative high-performing team will likely benefit an organization, and be a meaningful experience to the team members. Why? People want to be part of a strong team that works well together to resourcefully solve problems or build something new. When power is used for good, it attracts energy, life, and health. In contrast, coercive power is "actually a diminishment and distortion" of power (ibid., 10). When power is assumed to be a scarce zero-sum commodity, then one must fight to win and hoard power to protect one's status. Power-over behaviors often harm those who are targets of these tactics. If that is the case, then being subject to sustained power-over behavior may give rise to simmering resentment, subtle sabotage, or even more blatant power-from behaviors. Putting substantive effort into controlling coworkers' behavior is short-sighted and often backfires (Yukl 2013).

If the central meaning of power is "to be able" and we have a choice to use our power for good and *not* to harm, then the organizational values that undergird the use of power in organizations should embrace life-giving values. Bolman and Deal (2017, 216) state, "An organization can and should take a moral stance. It can make its values clear, hold employees accountable, and validate the need for dialogue about ethical choices." The values that guide our use of power in organizations are informed by our relationships, culture, organizational context, life experiences, etc. Of the many possible moorings that we could explore with regard to the use of power in organizations, two are briefly described in subsequent sections: valuing human dignity and valuing trustworthy character.

Valuing Human Dignity

Power used for common good embraces the value of human dignity. Each member of the organization deserves to be treated in a respectful manner. Understanding, articulating, and living the value of human dignity needs to be a clarion call for organizations who hope to use their power for good.

Whether it is recognized or not, dignity is an attribute that we are born with as human beings. Dignity "*is our inherent value and worth*" (Hicks 2018, 2). A "dignity consciousness" involves "a deep connection to our inherent value and worth and to the vulnerability that we all share to having our dignity violated" (ibid., 6). When we mutually honor one another's dignity, a sense of safety exists between us and "people feel free to make themselves vulnerable, free to reveal their true selves. Relationships thrive when both parties feel they are seen, heard, and valued" (3). However, having one's dignity violated unleashes "anger, resentment, and the desire for revenge" (9). Dignity violations often break trust and can destroy relationships. Within organizations, "A toxic workplace is one whose culture implicitly (and sometimes explicitly) condones dignity-violating behaviors. The unspoken norms enable hurtful interactions" (217).

We can unintentionally harm another coworker's dignity without even knowing it. Therefore, "we need to pay more attention to the effect we have on others. *Without dignity consciousness, even good people with good intentions can cause harm*" (85). To that end, Hicks (2018, 16–17) names "ten elements of dignity" as follows: "acceptance of identity," "recognition," "acknowledgement," "inclusion," "safety," "fairness," "independence," "understanding," "benefit of the doubt," and "accountability." When an organizational culture honors dignity, the members grow in appreciation for one another through the practice of these ten elements. However, in a toxic work environment, these elements are routinely violated. For example, the research of Hinks reports "Across all settings, the element of dignity that was violated the most was safety. *People did not feel safe to speak up to their bosses when they felt uncomfortable with the way they were being treated*" (85).

By contrast, when organizational cultures honor dignity, it "resides and flourishes in strong, mutually enhancing relationships" (98). Therefore "Leaders who understand the power of treating people well will see their people thrive, and they will thrive right along with them. Because when we honor others' dignity, we strengthen our own" (25). While, leaders need to embody and model honoring dignity, everyone is responsible to create a culture of dignity. We all need to learn how to honor dignity in ourselves and others. The skills needed to support a culture of dignity are "honor one's own and others' dignity"; "defend one's dignity with skill and humanity when necessary"; "give, receive, and ask for feedback"; "resolve conflict with dignity"; and "take responsibility for violating the dignity of others" (184). While learning to mutually honor one another's dignity is slow work, it is worth the investment of time (44). In the end, "The *acknowledgement* of the good in others promotes the *expression* of the good" (Curle 2007, 56).

Valuing Trustworthy Character

Trustworthy character is foundational to being a good leader. Bass and Bass (2008, 219) state, "The character of a leader involves his or her ethical and moral beliefs, intentions, and behavior." Hannah and Avolio (2011, 983) assert that "character is a (if not *the*) critical component of leadership." On a daily basis, leaders and organizational members put their values and beliefs into action. How a leader or organizational member uses power demonstrates the values that they hold. Sturm and Antonakis (2015, 149) observe that "power represents a double-edged sword; it can lead to both prosocial and antisocial outcomes depending on who the power holders are" and the context in which their power is exercised.

If a person's values are self-centered, their actions will primarily promote self-advantage. For example, a leader who values self-protection may exhibit controlling or micromanaging behaviors. Likewise, "Self-protective leadership is characterized by self-centeredness, elitism, status consciousness, narcissism, and a tendency to induce conflict with others" (House 2004, 7). Not surprising that "Self-protective leadership is generally reported to impede outstanding leadership" (Javidan et al. 2006, 73). As seen previously, when human dignity is violated, there are repercussions. By contrast, a person of trustworthy character honors the dignity of others. Kouzes and Posner (2017, 18) observe "Focusing on serving others' needs rather than one's own builds trust in a leader. The more people trust their leaders, and each other, the more they take risks, make changes, and keep moving ahead."

How do leaders of trustworthy character handle power? Trustworthy leaders do not hoard power, they collaboratively grow power. They are "concerned with neither granting power nor grabbing power but with evolving power" (Follett 1924, 188). In other words, "Genuine power can only be grown, it will slip from every arbitrary hand that grasps it; for genuine power is not coercive control, but coactive control" (ibid., xiii). Likewise, Crouch (2013, 41) observes "true power multiplies when it is shared." Mutual trust is essential to coactively growing power. We will look briefly at some leader behaviors that communicate trust, and behaviors that cultivate trust among organizational members.

Trust is built when a leader keeps their promises and when their words and deeds are consistent. When trying to decide whether or not "a leader is believable, people first listen to the words, then they watch the actions" (Kouzes and Posner 2017, 43). Over decades of research, being "*honest* still remains the number-one quality people look for in a person they would willingly follow" (ibid., 38). As a corollary, people do not want to follow a dishonest leader because it causes too much stress (33). Why? You cannot trust a dishonest person; the relationship is unsafe. Stated positively, "People must be able, above all else, to believe in their leaders. To *willingly* follow them, people must believe that the leaders' word can be trusted, that they are personally passionate and enthusiastic about their work, and that they have the knowledge and skill to lead" (40). In speaking about trustworthy behavior, it is also necessary to point out that the nuances of one's context and culture matter greatly. Having discernment and wisdom to know what behavior nurtures trusting relationships in a particular setting is crucial.

If an organizational culture embraces the notion of coactive power, then mutual trust among members is needed. Leaders must model trustworthy behavior and nurture trust in daily life. Zak (2017, 88–90) reports eight management behaviors that nurture trust: "recognize excellence," "induce challenge stress," "give people discretion in how they work," "enable job crafting," "share information broadly," "intentionally build relationships," "facilitate whole-person growth," and "show vulnerability." The benefits of nurturing trust are clear; employees "are more productive, have more energy at work, collaborate better with their colleagues, and stay with their employers longer than people working at low-trust companies. They also suffer less chronic stress and are happier with their lives, and these factors fuel stronger performance" (ibid., 86). Power can be used for good or for harm. Those who desire to use power for good will likely resonate with valuing human dignity and valuing trustworthy character.

Discussion Questions

- Regarding power in organizations, Follett (1924, 180) asked, "Is power force, influence, leadership, manipulation, managing, is it self-control, self-discipline, is it capacity, is it self-expression?" What is your understanding of power?
- How would you describe the use of power in your context? What modes of power are used? How do people access power? What behavior is rewarded? Punished? Ignored?
- What do you think about the terms "influence agent" and "target of influence" used in the literature to describe actors in a power exchange? What might be an alternative?
- In your experience, what motivates people to use power? How do they use their agency?
- In general, what are the potential negative or positive impacts of power on human dignity?
- In what ways can power be used to build organizational trust among members?

The Case of the Insecure Boss

Ryan is a young high potential CPA who has worked on an accounting team in a manufacturing company for three years. Ryan is one of four CPAs and more than twenty clerks that serve on the accounting team. Recently, the well-respected Director of Accounting, who hired Ryan, retired. The new Accounting Director, Shawn, was an external hire. Shawn quickly realized and was threatened by the fact that Ryan is a very talented accountant and highly regarded by his teammates. Almost from the start, Shawn treated Ryan differently than the other accountants. For example, Shawn frequently interrupts Ryan and criticizes him in front of other coworkers. He consistently gives Ryan a heavier workload than anyone else on the team. Ryan is growing frustrated and calls you to discuss the tense situation at work.

- How would you explore this with Ryan?
- What specific questions would you ask to unpack the situation?
- What power-over tactics is Shawn using?
- How would you help Ryan discern what to do regarding Shawn's power-over tactics?
- What actions would you encourage him to take? Or not take?
- How would you check in to see how this is impacting Ryan's sense of dignity?

References

Anderson, Cameron, and Sebastien Brion. 2014. "Perspectives on Power in Organizations." *Annual Review of Organizational Psychology and Organizational Behavior* 1: 67–97. https://doi.org/10.1146/annurev-orgpsych-031413-091259

Bacharach, Samuel B., and Edward J. Lawler. 1980. *Power and Politics in Organizations*. San Francisco: Jossey-Bass.

Bass, Bernard M., and Ruth Bass. 2008. *The Bass Handbook of Leadership: Theory, Research, and Managerial Applications*. 4th ed. New York: Free Press.

Bolman, Lee G., and Terrence E. Deal. 2017. *Reframing Organizations: Artistry, Choice, and Leadership*. 6th ed. Hoboken: Wiley.

Brass, Daniel J., and Marlene E. Burkhardt. 1993. "Potential Power and Power Use: An Investigation of Structure and Behavior." *Academy of Management Journal* 36 (3): 441–70.

Brass, Daniel J., and David M. Krackhardt. 2012. "Power, Politics, and Social Networks in Organizations." In *Politics in Organizations: Theory and Research Considerations*. Edited by Gerald R. Ferris and Darren C. Treadway, 355–75. New York: Routledge.

Carl, Dale, Vipin Gupta, and Mansour Javidan. 2004. "Power Distance." In *Culture, Leadership, and Organizations: The GLOBE Study of 62 Societies*, edited by Robert J. House, Paul J. Hanges, Mansour Javidan, Peter W. Dorfman, and Vipin Gupta, 513–63. Thousand Oaks: SAGE Publications.

Caza, Brianna Barker, Larissa Tiedens, and Fiona Lee. 2011. "Power Becomes You: The Effects of Implicit and Explicit Power on the Self." *Organizational Behavior and Human Decision Processes* 114 (1): 15–24. https://doi.org/10.1016/j.obhdp.2010.09.003

Clegg, Stewart R. 1989. "Radical Revisions: Power, Discipline and Organizations." *OrganizationStudies*10(1):97–115.https://doi.org/10.1177/017084068901000106

Clegg, Stewart R., David Courpasson, and Nelson X. Phillips. 2011. *Power and Organizations*. London: SAGE Publications.

Crouch, Andy. 2013. *Playing God: Redeeming the Gift of Power*. Downers Grove: IVP Books.

Curle, Adam. 2007. *True Justice: Quaker Peace Makers and Peace Making*. London: Quaker Books.

Dahl, Robert A. 1957. "The Concept of Power." *Behavioral Science* 2: 201–15. https://doi.org/10.1002/bs.3830020303

Daniels, Michael A., and Gary J. Greguras. 2014. "Exploring the Nature of Power Distance: Implications for Micro- and Macro-Level Theories, Processes, and Outcomes." *Journal of Management* 40 (5): 1202–29. https://doi.org/10.1177/0149206314527131

Emerson, Richard M. 1962. "Power-Dependence Relations." *American Sociological Review* 27 (1): 31–41.

Fairholm, Gilbert W. 2009. *Organizational Power Politics: Tactics in Organizational Leadership*. 2nd ed. Santa Barbara: Praeger.

Fleming, Peter, and André Spicer. 2014. "Power in Management and Organization Science." *Academy of Management Annals* 8 (1): 237–98. https://doi.org/10.5465/19416520.2014.875671

Follett, Mary Parker. 1924. *Creative Experience*. New York: Longmans, Green & Co.

———. [1925] 2013. *Dynamic Administration: The Collected Papers of Mary Parker Follett*. Illustrated ed. Mansfield Centre: Martino Fine Books.

French, John R. P. Jr., and Bertram Raven. 1959. "The Bases of Social Power." In *Studies in Social Power*. Edited by Dorwin Cartwright, 150–67. Ann Arbor: Institute for Social Research.

Habermas, Thomas McCarthy Jurgen. 1987. *The Theory of Communicative Action, Volume 2: Lifeworld and System: A Critique of Functionalist Reason*. Boston: Beacon Press.

Hannah, S. T., and B. J. Avolio. 2011. "The Locus of Leader Character." *The Leadership Quarterly* 22 (5): 979–83. https://doi.org/10.1016/j.leaqua.2011.07.016

Hardy, Cynthia. 1985. "The Nature of Unobtrusive Power." *Journal of Management Studies* 22 (4): 384–99. https://doi.org/10.1111/j.1467-6486.1985.tb00004.x

Hicks, Donna. 2018. *Leading with Dignity: How to Create a Culture That Brings Out the Best in People*. New Haven: Yale University Press.

Hofstede, Geert, and Gert Jan Hofstede. 2005. *Cultures and Organizations: Software of the Mind*. 2nd ed. New York: McGraw-Hill Education.

Hollander, Edwin P., and Lynn R. Offermann. 1990. "Power and Leadership in Organizations: Relationships in Transition." *American Psychologist, Organizational Psychology* 45 (2): 179–89. https://doi.org/10.1037/0003-066X.45.2.179

House, Robert J. 2004. "Illustrative Examples of GLOBE Findings." In *Culture, Leadership, and Organizations: The GLOBE Study of 62 Societies*. Edited by Robert J. House, Paul J. Hanges, Mansour Javidan, Peter W. Dorfman, and Vipin Gupta, 1–7. Thousand Oaks: SAGE Publications.

House, Robert J., and Mansour Javidan. 2004. "Overview of GLOBE." In *Culture, Leadership, and Organizations: The GLOBE Study of 62 Societies*. Edited by Robert J. House, Paul J. Hanges, Mansour Javidan, Peter W. Dorfman, and Vipin Gupta, 9–28. Thousand Oaks: SAGE Publications.

Javidan, Mansour, Peter W. Dorfman, Mary Sully de Luque, and Robert J. House. 2006. "In the Eye of the Beholder: Cross Cultural Lessons in Leadership from Project GLOBE." *The Academy of Management Perspectives* 20 (1): 67–90. https://doi.org/10.5465/AMP.2006.19873410

Kilduff, Martin, and Wenpen Tsai. 2003. *Social Networks and Organizations*. Thousand Oaks: SAGE Publications.

Kipnis, David, Stuart M. Schmidt, and Ian Wilkinson. 1980. "Intraorganizational Influence Tactics: Explorations in Getting One's Way." *Journal of Applied Psychology* 65 (4): 440–52. https://doi.org/10.1037/0021-9010.65.4.440

Kouzes, James M., and Barry Z. Posner. 2017. *The Leadership Challenge: How to Make Extraordinary Things Happen in Organizations*. 6th ed. Hoboken: Wiley.

McClelland, David C. 1970. "The Two Faces of Power." *Journal of International Affairs* 24 (1): 29–47.

McClelland, David C., and David H. Burnham. [1976] 2003. "Power Is the Great Motivator." *Harvard Business Review* 81 (1): 117–26.

McGregor, Douglas. [1960] 2006. *The Human Side of Enterprise*. Annotated ed. New York: McGraw-Hill.

Mendenhall, Mark E., Joyce Osland, Allan Bird, Gary R. Oddou, Michael J. Stevens, Martha Maznevski, and Günter K. Stahl, eds. 2018. *Global Leadership*. 3rd ed. New York: Routledge.

Mintzberg, Henry. 1983. *Power in and Around Organizations*. Englewood Cliffs: Prentice-Hall.

———. 1984. "Power and Organization Life Cycles." *Academy of Management Review* 9 (2): 207–24.

Northouse, Peter G. 2021. *Introduction to Leadership: Concepts and Practice*. 5th ed. Thousand Oaks: SAGE Publications.

Parsons, Talcott. 1963a. "On the Concept of Influence." *Public Opinion Quarterly* 27 (1): 37–62. https://doi.org/10.1086/267148

———. 1963b. "On the Concept of Political Power." *Proceedings of the American Philosophical Society* 107 (3): 232–62.

Pettigrew, Andrew M. 1972. "Information Control as a Power Resource." *Sociology* 6 (2): 187–204. https://doi.org/10.1177/003803857200600202

Pfeffer, Jeffrey. 1992. *Managing with Power: Politics and Influence in Organizations*. Reprint ed. Boston: Harvard Business Review Press.

———. 1997. *New Directions for Organization Theory: Problems and Prospects*. Oxford: Oxford University Press.

———. 2010. *Power: Why Some People Have It and Others Don't*. New York: Harper Business.

———. 2013. "You're Still the Same: Why Theories of Power Hold over Time and across Contexts." *The Academy of Management Perspectives* 27 (4): 269–80. https://doi.org/10.5465/amp.2013.0040

Raven, Bertram H. 1965. "Social Influence and Power." In *Current Studies in Social Psychology*, edited by Ivan Steiner and Martin Fishbein, 371–82. New York: Holt, Rinehart and Winston.

———. 1992. "A Power/Interaction Model of Interpersonal Influence: French and Raven Thirty Years Later." *Journal of Social Behavior & Personality* 7 (2): 217–44.

———. 2008. "The Bases of Power and the Power/Interaction Model of Interpersonal Influence." *Analyses of Social Issues & Public Policy* 8 (1): 1–22. https://doi.org/10.1111/j.1530-2415.2008.00159.x

Silber, John R. 1979. "The Conceptual Structure of Power: A Review." In *Power, Its Nature, Its Use, and Its Limits*. Edited by Donald W. Harward, 189–207. Boston: G.K. Hall.

Student, Kurt R. 1968. "Supervisory Influence and Work-Group Performance." *Journal of Applied Psychology* 52 (3): 188–94. https://doi.org/10.1037/h0025886

Sturm, Rachel E., and John Antonakis. 2015. "Interpersonal Power: A Review, Critique, and Research Agenda." *Journal of Management* 41 (1): 136–63. https://doi.org/10.1177/0149206314555769

Taylor, Frederick W. 1911. *The Principles of Scientific Management*. New York: Harper & Brothers Publishers.

VeneKlasen, Lisa, and Valerie Miller. 2007. *A New Weave of Power, People, and Politics: The Action Guide for Advocacy and Citizen Participation*. Warwickshire: Practical Action.

Weber, Max. 2012. *The Theory of Social and Economic Organization*. Edited by Talcott Parsons. Mansfield Centre: Martino Fine Books.

Wolff, Hans-Georg, and Klaus Moser. 2009. "Effects of Networking on Career Success: A Longitudinal Study." *Journal of Applied Psychology* 94 (1): 196–206. https://doi.org/10.1037/a0013350

Yukl, Gary. 2013. *Leadership in Organizations*. 8th ed. Boston: Pearson.

Yukl, Gary, and J. Bruce Tracey. 1992. "Consequences of Influence Tactics Used with Subordinates, Peers, and the Boss." *Journal of Applied Psychology* 77 (4): 525–35. https://doi.org/10.1037/0021-9010.77.4.525

Zak, Paul. 2017. "The Neuroscience of Trust." *Harvard Business Review* 95 (1): 84–90.

5 Change

Introduction

What is involved in organizational change? Is organizational change an event, a planned process, or constantly unfolding? Are these perspectives on change mutually exclusive? Is one perspective more prevalent than the others in practice? What kind of systems support each of these perspectives? What are the possible goals, outcomes, or purposes of each? What are the roles of the leader and organizational member? Organizational change has been described using each of these perspectives. We will investigate these perspectives and a variety of topics about organizational change on the balcony, on the road, and with attention to moorings.

Views From the Balcony

The balcony brings a necessary perspective when navigating change. Stepping back and considering new frameworks will stretch and help us better navigate the organizational road. On the balcony, we explore four organization archetypes that provide insight on the evolution of organizations. The archetypes are described using four metaphors. Understanding these archetype organizations gives background to explore a variety of organizational change models.

Evolving Organization Metaphors

"Every organizational form is a product of its era. This means that every organization must adapt to the conditions of its times" (Snow 2015, 435). We begin with four organization archetypes described through the lens of metaphor: the machine, the organism, the "human brain" (Morgan 2006, 223), and the "energy wave" (Colwill 2010, 114). These archetypes provide insight on the evolution of organizations. A caution should be noted.

DOI: 10.4324/9780429323959-5

Metaphors are "filters that screen some details and emphasize others" (Barrett and Cooperrider 1990, 222). In other words, "metaphors paradoxically expand one's perspective while at the same time limit the scope of what is seen" (Colwill 2010, 115). In naming these organizational metaphors, some aspects are emphasized and some are not. The main reason for their inclusion in this chapter is that understanding these archetype organizations gives background to explore a variety of organizational change models. Although some of these organizational forms have a longer history of use than others, they are all still represented in organizations today.

The Machine

The organization as machine arose during the industrial revolution. At this time, there was considerable growth in manufacturing companies supported by the disciplines of economics and engineering. Theorists taught that "management is a process of planning, organization, command, coordination, and control" (Morgan 2006, 18).

To paint the metaphorical picture, a machine is an apparatus with separate but interconnected parts that function together in performing a particular kind of work. A smooth-running machine maximizes efficiency and production. If a belt or pulley breaks, it must be quickly repaired or replaced to restore operations. The same functional logic was applied to the management of organizations through the use of hierarchical accountability structures, formal positions of authority, and prescribed roles for workers. Metaphorically, the belts and pulleys are the individual workers who perform specific functions in compliance with the overall system.

In the machine organization, if conflicts or problems arose, then the rationale was to identify the problem, analyze the cause, evaluate possible solutions, and develop action plans to implement the solution (Cooperrider et al. 2008). Stable environments offer the best chance of survival for bureaucratic organizations, since the highly structured and closed nature of mechanistic organizations creates difficulty in adapting to changing environmental circumstances. This lack of adaptability provided opportunity for the emergence of the organism organization.

The Organism

The inability of mechanistic organizations to respond to the external environment propelled people toward a different organizational model. Could it be that organizations are actually living systems? To investigate this, theorists turned to the field of ecology which deals with the relationships between organisms and their environments. Applied to organizations, the "social ecology" (Morgan 2006, 34) describes the living system of dynamic relationships and the environmental ecosystem of the organization.

Understanding the needs and vulnerabilities of an organism is essential for its survival in the wild. Likewise, organism organizations are open systems influenced by their need to survive and adapt in a competitive environment. With a "survival of the fittest" mentality, leaders strive to cultivate the health of the organization and protect it from threat. Effective leaders are participative and democratic; they encourage development of organizational members so the system will grow strong and thrive. Concern for the needs of employees is demonstrated by developing motivating jobs with autonomy, responsibility, and recognition (Morgan 2006). In organism organizations, the members are treated as valuable resources to the system.

The open system of organism organizations allowed for a better chance of survival in a competitive environment than the machine organization. However, the main criticism of organism organizations is that they are too dependent on the outside pressures of the external environment as motivation for change (Morgan 2006). The realization that people can be active participants in their own learning awakened the push toward the human brain organization.

The Human Brain

The transition from the industrial age toward the information age brought with it many changes to the leadership and management of organizations (Colwill 2010). With the influx of information and technology, a very different organizational model was needed. Organizations not only needed to learn about and respond to their external environments, they also needed to improve their intraorganizational learning to stay competitive. The organization as "human brain" (Morgan 2006) entered the arena. In the same way, the brain is the information processing center for the human body, the brain organization highlights the use of internal learning within its own self-organized system. Organizational learning addresses "how organizations can be designed to promote effective learning processes and how those learning processes themselves can be improved. An organization designed to promote learning can create a continuous stream of valuable knowledge" (Cummings and Worley 2008, 556).

Whereas the organism organization used a "functionalist" organizational learning paradigm that focuses on learning how to adapt to the external environment, the human brain organization garners a "constructionist" perspective, and "constructionists turn their lens inside organizations and examine specific activities, situations, and cultures where organizational learning is situated" (Popova-Nowak and Cseh 2015, 318). As such, "new information becomes knowledge when it is socially negotiated, interpreted, and shared within the organization" (ibid., 316). The process of engaging in the everyday practices with coworkers provides "a way for individuals to acquire, produce, reproduce, and expand organizational knowledge" (317).

The "learning organization" is one example of a human brain organization (Morgan 2006). Senge's ([1990] 2006) work envisions a learning organization comprised of five disciplines: systems thinking, personal mastery, mental models, shared vision, and team learning. Learning organizations seek to enable people to rise above cognitive biases through systems thinking. Systems thinking is a mindset for seeing detail, patterns, and interrelationships, while also looking at the whole. Leaders facilitate learning by engaging "knowledge workers" in dialogue about issues that are crucial to the organization's development (ibid., 18). They foster ongoing ability to collectively learn and overcome organizational "learning disabilities" (18). Argyris (1999, 6) finds some value in the "learning organization" framework but contends that little attention is paid to the "processes that threaten the validity or utility of organizational learning" nor does it deal with "the difficulties of implementation." Morgan (2006) adds that a major limitation of the learning organization framework is that it is difficult time-consuming work and often elusive. Human brain organizations make collaborative learning a central feature in order to improve performance. Knowledge is collaboratively generated and responsibly acted upon.

The Energy Wave

The information age brought forth the human brain organization which engaged collaborative learning as its competitive advantage. Building on this collaborative foundation, some organizations sought to apply their energy toward deliberately focusing on the common good. Arising from quantum thought, the concept of an "energy wave" could be used as a metaphor to describe this type of fluid postmodern organization (Colwill 2010). An organization shaped by the principles and practices of appreciative inquiry is an example of an energy wave organization. Appreciative inquiry "is an organization development process and approach to change management that grows out of social constructionist thought and its applications to management and organizational transformation" (Cooperrider et al. 2008, 2).

Let's briefly unpack the energy wave itself. Newtonian physics described the world in terms of time, space, energy, matter, and causation (Colwill 2010). In this view, an entity is *either* a particle or an energy wave, one or the other but not both (Zohar 1997). In contrast, quantum physics teaches that a physical entity which appears to be a solid actually has both particle-like and wave-like properties. This concept from quantum physics can be used as an analogy to describe the appreciative organization. The particle-like aspects illustrate the daily practices of appreciative inquiry, whereas the wave-like aspects represent the principles and guiding forces or life-giving energy of an appreciative organization (Colwill 2010). The particle-like and wave-like features of appreciative organizations are briefly explored in the following text to illustrate the energy wave organization.

The particle-like view of appreciative organizations represents the on-the-ground aspects of daily practice. The leader of an appreciative organization is conceptualized as a designer (Avital 2008). They see through a "positive lens" and have the "capacity to construct better organizations and technologies through discourse that encourages human strengths and participative action in leading organizational change" (ibid., 3). Appreciative leaders foster a positive climate, cultivate affirming relationships, promote encouraging communication, expand vision through a spirit of inquiry, nurture positive meaning, and value authenticity (Cameron 2008; Colwill 2009).

The wave-like aspect of appreciative organizations is the discovery or unfolding of life-giving future possibilities and potential (Colwill 2010). Appreciative inquiry seeks to illuminate the "positive core" of an organization and build upon it (Cooperrider et al. 2008). In this view, organizational change is not about reducing obstacles or fixing problems. Rather, appreciative inquiry seeks to highlight the life-giving aspects of an organization in order to further stimulate and build upon this energy. In other words, appreciative inquiry "focuses on change through the identification of positive forces within an organization" (Sharkey, Yaeger, and Sorenson 2004, 521). These live-giving forces are the energy wave of the appreciative organization.

Popova-Nowak and Cseh (2015, 316) note, "For post-modernists, new information becomes knowledge when it becomes a part of organizational discourse." Appreciative inquiry assumes that the shared interactions and experiences of the organizational members have a primary influence on shaping the organization itself (Cummings and Worley 2008). In other words, undergirding appreciative inquiry is the belief that people have the collective ability to influence their own future (Seo, Putnam, and Bartunek 2004). This belief is "apparent in the overt choice of various humanistic means and processes in initiating organizational change, such as stories, narratives and visions" (ibid., 97). Interconnected participation of organizational members and leaders in large group meetings cultivates life-giving themes selected from the stories people share. Inquiry is initiated around the themes which leads to articulating innovative avenues of realizing a preferred future state. Throughout the process, energy is gained by focusing on what is life-giving within the organizational community and beyond.

However, like any change intervention, if appreciative inquiry is not supported with strong follow through, people may generate positive ideas, have great plans, but have no way to express them. The resultant disappointment will lead to frustration, and frustration to skepticism (Bushe 1999). Another concern is that the focus on positive stories might marginalize those who have negative experiences that could be important and meaningful to share (Bushe 2011).

As their thoughts have matured regarding appreciative inquiry, Cooperrider and Fry (2020) speak about three levels of appreciative inquiry. The lowest and easiest level is "AI into the extraordinary" (ibid., 268). The second, more difficult level is "AI during times of the ordinary" (268). The third and elevated level of AI capacity "is not AI into moments of excellence nor is it about meaning making in the ordinary, but AI in the midst of tragedy" (269). They state, "The task of AI is the penetrating search for what gives life, what fuels developmental potential, and what has deep meaning—even in the midst of the tragic" (269). In any case, appreciative inquiry is challenging and will require leaders who are skilled, wise, and discerning.

As stated earlier, all these metaphorical archetypes are still in operation. Table 5.1 offers a summary of the four metaphors. The context, culture,

Table 5.1 Summary of four metaphors.

Guiding metaphor	Machine	Organism	Brain	Energy wave
Type of organization	Bureaucratic	Open system	Learning	Appreciative
View of organizational process	Mechanistic	Social ecology	Self-organizing	Unfolding
Predominant change process	Reacting	Redesigning	Reframing	Regenerating
Preferred outcome of change	Maximizes production	Survival, adaptation	Knowledge is generated and acted upon	Positive potential is being realized
Level of learning	Action, task	Dynamic interrelationships	Cognition and action	Innovation and creativity
Organizational values	Efficiency, production, control	Health and development	Collaborative learning	Interconnected participation
Role of leadership	Commander, director	Participative, democratic	Facilitator	Architect, designer
Role of organizational members	Skilled workers	Valuable resources	Knowledge workers	Collaborators

industry, and people involved would specify which of these metaphors could be appropriate. Other organization metaphors have been named (Morgan 2006). With this brief look at four archetype organizations, we must consider that one model of organizational change cannot possibly encompass the breadth of all these forms. The evolution of organizations naturally influenced change efforts.

A Continuum of Change Models

Hughes (2019, 18) states "no consensus definition of organizational change exists" and "there can never be one best way to make change happen, there cannot be one best way to classify/study organizational change" (ibid., 28). These words provide both freedom and caution. The freedom is that there are many ways to engage organizational change. The caution is that it is dangerous to assert that one type of change fits all situations. With this caution in mind and realizing that there are many other approaches that could have been named here, we will look at a continuum of organizational change models.

Directed Change

Directed change is driven and controlled from the top of the organizational pyramid. It "involves a tightly defined, unchanging goal, as well as a clearly defined and constrained change process" (Kerber and Buono 2018, 2). Moreover, "Leaders create and announce the change and seek to convince organizational members to accept it based on business necessity, logical arguments (rational persuasion), emotional appeals, and the leader's credibility" (ibid., 7). In short, this type of change "relies on authority, persuasion, and compliance" (7). The advantage is that change is initiated quickly and decisively (7). A disadvantage when used "inappropriately, organizational members are forced to cope with the well-known reactions of the recipients of the imposed change—denial, anger, bargaining, sadness, and loss" (8). Directed change echoes the dynamics of power-over mode described in Chapter 4, and the structured hierarchical nature of the above-described machine organization.

Planned Change

Whereas directed change is controlled from the top, planned change is "flexible and participative, and the leader's role is to work with organizational members to devise a plan to accomplish the change goal" (Kerber and Buono 2018, 2). Planned change "starts slowly while the plan is created so that the process can move more quickly once implementation begins" (ibid., 2). Cummings and Worley (2008, 23) state "Organizations can use planned change to solve problems, to learn from experience, to reframe shared perceptions, to adapt to external environmental changes, to improve performance, and to influence future changes."

Planned change "provides a 'roadmap.' It attempts to create the conditions for key stakeholders to become more involved in both the form and implementation of the change" (Buono and Kerber 2010, 7). These authors point out that most planned change models are undergirded by Kurt Lewin's "three-stage process of unfreezing, changing, and refreezing: (1) unfreezing or releasing the organization from its current patterns, (2) transitioning the resulting, more malleable, organization from its current patterns to more adaptive ones, and then (3) refreezing the organization into a new set of patterns by weaving them into the fabric of the organization" (ibid., 7).

Hughes (2019, 168) observes a similarity between Lewin's model described previously and Kotter's ([1996] 2012) eight-step planned change model: establishing a sense of urgency, creating the guiding coalition, developing a vision and strategy, communicating the change vision, empowering employees for broad-based action, generating short-term wins, consolidating gains and producing more change, and anchoring new approaches in the culture. Kotter's model is based on his consulting experience, not upon research, nor upon cited literature (Hughes 2016). The main critique of Kotter's model is the lack of evidential support for the model (Hughes 2019). Other critiques include employees are depicted as change resisters; dynamics of ethics, power, and politics are underplayed; linear step sequence is overemphasized; organizational history is ignored limiting learning from the past and lacking an appreciation of incremental change; the leader and leader's communication are overemphasized; unique cultural contexts are underemphasized; and evaluation of change efforts as either success or failure is overly simplistic (ibid., 167).

Not all planned change takes this "one-size-fits-all" form but many of the critiques leveled by Hughes (2019) could apply to planned change efforts if they are not seriously heeded or if the process itself is handled inappropriately. Buono and Kerber (2010, 8) note if planned change is used inappropriately, it can "result in significant reductions in productivity, overwhelm organizational members with its complexity, and alienate key stakeholders as a result of limited participation and influence in the process." In addition, leaders are overly burdened with initiating and sustaining change (ibid., 8). Planned change has some of the same dynamics as power-over or power-to modes described in Chapter 4. It also aligns with the organism organization, and some elements of the abovementioned human brain organization.

Iterative Changing

Whereas directed change is controlled from the top, and planned change is a road map to follow, "*iterative changing* is an improvisational, almost experimental process focused on a loosely defined direction rather than a clear change goal" (Kerber and Buono 2018, 2). Leaders coach and guide collaboration "to identify both the goal of the change as well as the process to get there" (ibid., 2). The aligning factor is commitment to the organization's shared purpose and values (Hill et al. 2014). This fluid approach to change can be effective in organizations that require learning and innovation as their mainstay (Colwill 2010). Moreover, "this approach attempts to take full advantage of the expertise and creativity of organizational members, reconfiguring existing practices and models and testing new ideas and perspectives" (Buono and Kerber 2010, 8). Likewise, "innovation and development contribute to both continuous improvement of existing change efforts as well as the ability to generate novel changes and solutions" (ibid., 8). However, if used inappropriately, it "can contribute to organizational chaos, as continuous changes and transitions confuse and frustrate rather than enlighten organizational members and other key stakeholders" (8). Another potential disadvantage is repeated iterations can consume time and energy with little tangible benefit (8). Iterative changing echoes the dynamics of power-with mode described in Chapter 4 as well as some aspects of the human brain and energy wave organizations described earlier.

Using the change model continuum provides flexibility to choose the appropriate model depending on the complexity and uncertainty of the situation. Buono and Kerber (2010, 5) advocate moving from "change readiness" to "change capacity." Change readiness is the ability to "reflect and recognize the need for a particular change at a specific point in time" (4). Whereas "change capacity is the ability of an organization to change not just once, but as a normal response to changes in its environment" (5).

Process Theories of Change

Process theories of change describe the unfolding nature of organizational change. Van de Ven and Poole (1995, 511) named four process theories of organizational change: "life cycle, teleology, dialectical, and evolutionary." These change models explain "how and why change unfolds" (ibid., 511). Ideally, taken together, these theories depict an interplay between different perspectives which "helps one gain a more comprehensive understanding of organizational life, because one theoretical perspective invariably offers only a partial account of a complex phenomenon" (511). Each change theory will be briefly described in the following paragraphs.

The life cycle theory follows "a single sequence of stages or phases" (515). The idea is analogous to the life cycle of living organisms. The "characteristics acquired in earlier stages are retained in later stages" and the stages "derive from a common underlying process" (515). The "key metaphor" is "organic growth" and this growth has a "linear and irreversible sequence of prescribed stages" (514). According to this theory, organizations eventually reach a stage of decline (Hughes 2019).

Telos is the Greek word for "end, purpose, or goal"; therefore, the "teleological" theory of change is driven by "the philosophical doctrine that purpose or goal is the final cause for guiding movement of an entity" (516). Organizations aim at reaching full potential of their inherent purpose. The "key metaphor" is "purposeful cooperation" (514). This model "views development as a cycle of goal formulation, implementation, evaluation, and modification of goals based on what was learned by the entity. This sequence emerges through the purposeful social construction among individuals within the entity" (520).

Van de Ven and Sun (2011, 63) state "Dialectical theories explain stability and change in terms of the relative balance of power between opposing entities. Stability is produced through struggles and accommodations that maintain the status quo between oppositions. Change occurs when challengers gain sufficient power to confront and engage incumbents." In this model, "confrontation and conflict between opposing entities generate this dialectical cycle" (Van de Ven and Poole 1995, 521).

The evolutionary model of "development consists of a repetitive sequence of variation, selection, and retention events among entities in a designated population. Competition for scarce environmental resources between entities inhabiting a population generates this evolutionary cycle" (ibid., 521). The "key metaphor" is "competitive survival" (514).

These theories bring "contrasting worldviews of social change and development" applied to organizations (511). Van de Ven and Sun (2011, 71) state "organizational change can become more strategic and less myopic by increasing one's repertoire of alternative models of change. Any single mental model provides only a partial account of complex processes." Hughes (2019, 23) notes, "these theories are particularly useful in explaining sequences of change events."

Life Along the Road

The balcony briefly described the shifting nature of organizations and their approaches to organizational change. We now turn to the organizational road. First, we briefly consider the impact of these shifts on the roles of organizational leaders and members. Next, we explore two essential elements for organizational change: ability and willingness. Third, the relationship between resistance and change is discussed, followed by common pitfalls in leading change. The last topic is managing transitions during change.

Evolving Organizational Roles

Leaders and organizational members have been impacted by the evolution of organizations. Using the organization metaphor framework, the evolving role of leaders moves from commander or director of the machine organization, to participative democratic leader in the organism organization, to learning facilitator in the human brain organization, to architect or designer in the energy wave organization (Colwill 2010). Likewise, the role of organizational members is evolving from skilled worker, to valuable resource, to knowledge worker, to collaborator. Table 5.1 offers a summary of these shifting roles and they are briefly described in the following text.

In the machine organization, the leader as commander uses a directed change model to implement organizational change. Argyris (1999, 83) observes "the three underlying assumptions of formal pyramidal structure are specialization of work, unity of command, and centralization of power." As described in Chapter 4, "legitimate power" based on hierarchical position is leveraged to direct organizational efforts; and, if necessary, this position power is augmented by coercive power-over tactics to achieve compliance. In this leader-centric model, the directives flow down the chain of command. One-way communication insulates top leaders from what is actually happening on the ground. The lack of two-way communication may result in poor decisions due to an incomplete picture of the system. Organizational members are viewed as skilled workers who have specific functions to play. Morgan (2006, 30) notes "The mechanistic approach to organization tends to limit rather than mobilize the development of human capacities, molding human beings to fit the requirements of mechanical organization rather than building the organization around their strengths and potentials." Deviations from prescribed roles are discouraged, resistance may be penalized, and compliance may be rewarded.

Organism organizations focus on promoting and protecting the health of the organization for its own survival. Leaders are actively engaged in what is happening in order to make better decisions and provide better guidance. Leaders ensure that communication flows upward and downward in the system realizing that cooperative work cannot be accomplished alone. Working together using a planned change model the organization aligns according to the road map for change. Therefore, leaders need to articulate compelling vision, shape a plan, motivate others to action, and promote the best interests of the organization and its members. To grow organizational capacity, leaders develop and promote employees who support the organization's health and growth. Broadly speaking, leaders encourage active involvement of all organizational members. Likewise, in the organism organization, "Particular attention is focused on the idea of making employees feel more useful and important by giving them meaningful jobs and by giving as much autonomy, responsibility, and recognition as possible as a means of getting them involved in their work" (Morgan 2006, 36). In short, employees are seen as valuable resources to the system. In the organism organization, the burden of initiating, leading, and sustaining planned change falls on the shoulders of leaders.

The human brain organization elevates learning as a primary capacity. Leaders are facilitators of learning. Knowledge is collaboratively generated and acted upon. Learning often happens in self-organizing teams. Thus, the brain organization is not as leader-centric as the machine or organism organizations. Moreover, "Any move away from hierarchically controlled structures toward more flexible, emergent patterns has major implications for the distribution of power and control within an organization, as the increase in autonomy granted to self-organizing units undermines the ability of those with ultimate power to keep a firm hand on day-to-day activities and development" (Morgan 2006, 114). Ideally, more ownership of the purpose and process is shared throughout the organization using a "teleological" change model where collaborative purpose is the driver. Collaboration is effective "when competent, mature individuals treat each other fairly and value their relationship as much as their own self-interest" (Snow 2015, 435). Organizational members are dependable knowledge workers who bring necessary expertise to the table "in which all the parties with a stake in the problem constructively explore their differences and develop a joint strategy for action" (ibid., 435).

The energy wave organization seeks to harness life-giving potential for the common good. As such, leaders are architects or designers that create a conducive environment for organizational members to dream together about what might be possible and then collectively carry it out. In short, leaders "shape the context in which others are willing and able to innovate" (Hill et al. 2014, 117). Change agency is shared and dispersed throughout an organization. Leaders and members actively interconnect as they participate in the mission of the organization. In the energy wave organization, both leaders and members are viewed as collaborators in unfolding the ongoing change.

Able and Willing

Challenging and worthwhile endeavors require the ability and willingness to do the job. Ability is having the skill or competence to accomplish something. Willingness is being prepared and committed to engage in the work. Being both able and willing are crucial to the practice of organizational change and innovation (Hill et al. 2014).

Change Abilities

Many skills or abilities could be named that foster organizational change. In the following paragraphs, we will explore the overarching change abilities of learning and conversing, followed by, four "routines of agility" (Worley, Williams, and Lawler 2014). These abilities may need to be adapted depending on the history, culture, industry, type of organization, and unique situation.

Learning is at the heart of change. How can you genuinely change without learning? And how can you deeply learn without changing? Kouzes and Posner (2016, 49) state "Learning is the master skill. When you fully engage in learning—when you throw yourself wholeheartedly into experimenting, reflecting, reading, or getting coaching—you're going to experience improvement." Organizational learning is a social process. If productive collaborative learning is desired, then, leaders and members must learn how to learn together. Learning is multifaceted. We learn by actively working together, reflecting on our experiences, mutually sharing information, building shared meaning, and gleaning wisdom from each other. By contrast, learning is stymied in highly competitive or over controlling environments. For example, in highly competitive organizations, if individuals have valuable information but selfishly don't share it with coworkers, this power-over tactic diminishes their coworkers' ability to learn. Likewise, in high-control settings, "If employees cannot make honest mistakes, they cannot learn. If great people cannot learn, they leave. If they leave, you cannot adapt" (Worley, Williams, and Lawler 2014, 101).

As a social process, organizational learning and change require robust conversations. For example, when learning or innovation is the goal, "rules of engagement" encourage psychologically safe climate (Hill et al. 2014, 109). These authors found that in contexts promoting innovation, rules of engagement guide how people interact and how they think (ibid., 109). Interaction rules involve cultivating "mutual trust," "mutual respect," and "mutual influence" (111). Whereas rules about how people think are "question everything," "be data driven," and "see the whole" (113). Rules of engagement promote "creative abrasion" which is "the ability to create a marketplace of ideas, to generate, refine, and evolve a multitude of options through discourse, debate, and even conflict" (118). Creative abrasion involves both "support and confrontation"; that is why it works "within a community built on purpose, values, and rules" (139). Learning and conversing are overarching organizational change abilities that need to be regularly practiced with one's colleagues.

In addition to learning and conversing, "routines of agility" are practiced in consistently high-performing organizations (Worley, Williams, and Lawler 2014, 27). Agility is "the ability to make timely, effective, and sustained change results from the capacity to *strategize* in dynamic ways, accurately *perceive* changes in the external environment, *test* possible responses, and *implement* changes in products, technology, operations, structures, systems, and capabilities as a whole" (ibid., 27). Moreover, "Agility is a high-order dynamic capability that is built over time on a solid foundation of good management practices and a set of differentiated capabilities that confer a competitive advantage" (28). The "high-order dynamic capability" is reflected in four routines of agility: strategizing, perceiving, testing, and implementing (27). The routines are briefly described as follows.

The strategizing routine "sets the context and establishes the frame for what the organization does and how it goes about doing it" (57). A comparable practice from Pasmore (2015, 46) is "deciding" which is the ability to "prioritize efforts to close the gap between the vision and current reality." Strategizing involves understanding the organizational context and mission, prioritizing its change efforts, and deciding how it will implement the efforts.

The perceiving routine "gathers, analyzes, transmits, and supports the interpretation of environmental information" (Worley, Williams, and Lawler 2014, 66). The organization pursues a clearer picture of their position in relation to what is going on in their environment. A related idea from Pasmore (2015, 46) is "discovering" in which you step back, scan, and identify viable opportunities. Perceiving is the ability to scan and digest the bigger picture from the organizational balcony.

The testing routine involves setting up a test, running it, and learning from it (Worley, Williams, and Lawler 2014). Hill et al. (2014, 118) name this "creative agility" or "the organizational ability to test and refine ideas through quick experiments, reflection, and adjustment." Pasmore (2015, 46) names "discerning" as the ability to "learn from experience to improve change capacity over time."

Implementing enables the "capacity to embed new responses, capabilities, and strategies in the organization" (Worley, Williams, and Lawler 2014, 110). This routine "also complements the other agility routines by keeping the existing organization running smoothly and maintaining the workforce capacity needed to adapt" (ibid., 110). Pasmore (2015, 46) describes this capacity as "doing" or the ability to "engage the organization in executing the change strategy."

Change Willingness

Willingness involves commitment and openness to engage in learning and change. Willingness is cultivated when people "feel part of a community engaged in something more important than any of them as individuals and larger than any could accomplish alone" (Hill et al. 2014, 91). People want to be a part of something that is worth their time and effort. They want to contribute to something that matters to them. Willingness grows when people share common interests and they see the benefits of working together. It grows when genuine care for coworkers is demonstrated.

Willingness is essential in the collaborative work of learning and change. Willingness is cultivated by creating a climate of trust, honesty, and transparency; where mutual support and relationships are a priority; and where establishing a sense of community and belonging is central. A climate of psychological safety creates an environment where people willingly participate and share what is important to them. Leaders need to model trustworthy behavior and listen to coworkers' concerns about the impact of change.

Resistance and Change

Many people assume that when change is initiated, it will be met with resistance. Anderson (2017, 187) notes there is "little agreement about a definition or set of behaviors that universally count as resistant." Yet, we all have encountered behaviors we might call "resistant." A closer look is warranted. First, we will consider some reasons people resist change. Next, we will explore a range of possible manager behaviors: blaming the resister, rethinking resistance, and finding the value of resistance.

Why People Resist

When change is imposed, especially through coercive power-over tactics, the environment is ripe for resistance. In other words, "People don't resist change, they resist being changed" (Spector 2013, 13). However, not all change efforts are heavy-handed power-over maneuvers, but people may still resist change efforts for a variety of reasons. Spector (2013, 12) reports several reasons people resist change: "they remain satisfied with the status quo"; "they view change as a personal threat"; "they see the cost of change outweighing the benefits"; "they believe that management is mishandling the process"; or, "they believe that the change effort is not likely to succeed."

Blaming the Resister

Managers respond in a variety of ways to perceived resistance to change. A common response is to blame the resister and react in some way against them. For instance, if managers are feeling threatened by perceived resistance, they "may become competitive, defensive, and uncommunicative, more concerned about being right, looking good (or not looking bad), and winning (having their way) than about accomplishing the change" (Ford and Ford 2009, 24). Managers may label behaviors they simply don't like as "resistance" regardless of whether or not the person is intentionally resisting (ibid., 24). This labeling pushes "the resister" to the sidelines. Blaming and labeling alienate "potential partners in accomplishing change by relating to them as obstacles rather than resources" (24). These reactions may "cost good will and valuable relationships as well as the opportunity to learn how to improve change implementation" (24).

Rethinking Resistance

Another response to perceived resistance is to pause, reflect, and rethink what is occurring. Hughes (2019, 167) advocates "rethinking resistance" as the "subtle and diverse responses to ongoing organizational change processes." When we understand "our inclination to dismiss certain behaviors as resistance, we can learn to listen in a new way to the opportunities those behaviors provide for a successful change" (Ford and Ford 2009, 24). Ironically, people labeled "resisters" are "unlikely to see their own behavior that way. On the contrary, people perceived as 'resisters' may believe their behaviors are consistent with and supportive of organization objectives or values" (ibid., 25). Leaders need to seek out and understand the reasons behind employee behavior and involve employees in change efforts "rather than marginalizing them as resistant bystanders" (Hughes 2019, 167).

Finding the Value of Resistance

A third manager response recognizes that "resistance has a value" (Ford and Ford 2009, 27). Spector (2013, 11) states, "Employee resistance is not just a negative force to be overcome; it also presents an opportunity to learn." Therefore, we need to encourage people to express themselves rather than marginalize or repress the "resister." Resistance may be a "legitimate response of engaged and committed people who want a voice in something that is important to them" (Ford and Ford 2009, 35). Engaging "resistant" communicators can deepen the change discussion as well as build involvement, engagement, and commitment to the organization (Anderson 2017).

Interpreting resistance as feedback, and "Working with people in an organization to clarify their concerns is a strategy for improving the success of change initiatives. Change planning and implementation can be made smarter, faster, and cheaper by listening to the feedback embedded in 'resistance'" (Ford and Ford 2009, 35).

Common Pitfalls in Leading Change

The mindset and behavior of leaders matter in navigating change. Wise change leadership is learned on the organizational road. An inexperienced leader may be in over their head when it comes to leading change. Therefore, it is misguided to delegate a difficult change initiative to an inexperienced person. Regardless of experience level, there are some common pitfalls in leading change: unfamiliarity with power dynamics, difficulty navigating conflict, overestimating the role of the leader, underestimating context and culture, short-sighted planning and implementation strategy, and lack of care for the ecosystem.

Hughes (2019, 180) reports, "power and politics are largely unacknowledged in organizational change theories and practices." This lack of awareness of power dynamics is unfortunate since organizational "change intensifies political behavior" (Buchanan and Badham 2008, 41). These authors strongly assert "the change agent who is not politically skilled will fail" (ibid., 18). Chapter 4 explores the dense forest of power, attempting to highlight some of what leaders and organizational members need to know and practice.

Another area that leaders may lack awareness is navigating conflict. There are many ways that a leader can mishandle conflict. For example, leaders who use only their default conflict style will hamper their ability to appropriately meet the situation. Case in point: conflict avoidant leaders who "seek to preserve harmony by muffling creative disagreement will limit the number of good options considered" (Hill et al. 2014, 119). Organizational change requires surfacing disagreements, engaging in productive task conflict, and exercising improved ways of thinking together. If leaders lack experience managing conflict or have not learned from experience, it will show. Chapter 3 explores organizational conflict.

Leaders may overestimate their own importance when implementing change initiatives. Hughes (2019, 6) observes "We appear to live in an age of change leadership persuaded and even seduced by the agency of exceptional change leaders to make change happen." The desire and push for a heroic leader to fix things sets the leader up to fail. Spector (2013, 161) warns that "Dominating individual leaders can actually hurt an organization's ability to change." Leaders "who exercise discipline and control by marching their groups directly to a predetermined solution will discourage the trial-and-error efforts that lead to the best answer" and "groups led by someone who believes it's the leader's job to make choices early and often are less likely to develop the most creative and thoughtful solutions" (Hill et al. 2014, 119). In short, we need to rethink leader-centric change models.

When engaging change in organizations, leaders may underestimate the importance of understanding their context and culture. Chapters 3 and 4 unpack some aspects of leadership and culture. Hughes (2019, 168) urges, "Rethinking a-contextual accounts of leading change, in favor of acknowledging unique contexts and cultures encourages movement away from formulaic recipes and refocuses upon the diverse choices reflexive change leaders have to make." A "common mistake" leaders make is "not adequately addressing the organization's culture as a major force directly influencing the success of change" (Anderson and Anderson 2010, 20). The aforementioned perceiving ability is needed for an organization to get a clearer balcony picture of what is occurring within its system and external environment.

Anderson and Anderson (2020, 20) name "common mistakes" that occur in planning and implementing change strategy. First, a change effort that has not been clearly linked to the purpose and overall strategy of the organization may lack "relevance and meaning" (ibid., 20). Second, "not providing clear change leadership roles, structure, and decision making" shows inadequate governance of change (20). Third, an organization may struggle with change if it has "no enterprise change agenda, no common change methodology, and inadequate infrastructure to execute change successfully" (20). Fourth, misdiagnosing the scope and magnitude of change is another common mistake (20).

A final potential pitfall is failing to care for the organizational ecosystem. Hill et al. (2014, 223) summarize it this way:

> Without a sense of community—of being pulled together by common purpose, shared values, and clear rules of engagement openly developed—an innovation ecosystem is likely to flounder. Without a leader who understands this and works diligently to build and sustain that sense, the ecosystem will likely remain a mere collection of players who cooperate and coordinate, not a community capable of breakthrough work.

In short, an anemic ecosystem is not conducive to change or innovation. By contrast, caring for the ecosystem means caring for the people, making sure they are not overworked, bored, or underchallenged. It means caring for the relationships and the interactions of coworkers. It means caring for the collaborative work and its contribution.

Managing Transitions

Another misstep in leading change is "not adequately or proactively attending to the emotional side of change; not designing actions to minimize negative emotional reactions; not attending to them in constructive ways once they occur" (Anderson and Anderson 2010, 20). In short, mishandling people's emotional reactions to change is a failure to manage transitions.

What is the difference between change and transition? According to Bridges and Bridges (2017, 3), change focuses on organizational outcomes, whereas transition "is psychological; it is a three-phase process that people go through as they internalize and come to terms with the details of the new situation that change brings about." The three phases are "ending or letting go," "the neutral zone," and "the new beginning" (5). The phases will be briefly explored as follows.

When change is initiated, people wrestle with "letting go of the old ways and the old identity they had. This first phase of transition is an ending and the time when you need to help people to deal with their losses" (5). Leaders need to listen to coworker's concerns and observe how the change is impacting them. Depending on the degree of impact, individuals may show signs of the grieving process: "denial, anger, bargaining, anxiety, sadness, disorientation, and depression" (33). An open and empathetic acknowledgment of their losses may be a helpful supportive response (31). Ongoing information updates are crucial; and, clearly defining what is ending and what isn't ending provides reassurance to employees (37).

The "neutral zone" is the "in-between time when the old is gone but the new isn't fully operational" (5). People often feel anxiety during this phase and need time to process the change. Therefore, leaders should not rush people through the neutral zone (9). Furthermore, "It is a time when reorientation and redefinition must take place" (49). Normalizing the neutral zone as a common response to organizational change may reduce some of the anxiety people feel during this phase (49). Once people have had some time to heal the losses that they have incurred, they will be more open to accept what is next.

The "new beginning" happens when people "develop the new identity, experience the new energy, and discover the new sense of purpose that makes the change begin to work" (5). It can only happen "after they have come through the wilderness and are ready to make the emotional commitment to do things the new way and see themselves as new people" (66). Leaders can reinforce new beginnings with congruent word and action (78). For example, if teamwork is the new way of operating, then rewarding teamwork fosters the new beginning. However, if the leader incongruently reinforces the old ways by rewarding individual performance, then that leader is working against new beginnings.

Transition gets tricky when undergoing several types of change initiatives at once or if you are in a sea of constant change. If that is the case, the authors suggest that you transition to "change as the norm" (116). In other words, "only if continuous change is normalized as the new status quo can it be assimilated" (117). Continual change is the new beginning.

Another tricky situation is dealing with "the aftermath of mismanaged or unmanaged transition" (152). The aftermath may or may not be caused by your mishandling of transition; you may have inherited the situation. There are tangible costs of not managing transition effectively. Five lingering costs are "guilt, resentment, anxiety, self-absorption, and stress" (153). It is not surprising that "The single biggest reason organizational changes fail is because no one has thought about endings or planned to manage their impact on people" (42). When initiating change, the wise leader will remember that "transition begins with an ending and finishes with a beginning" (5).

Focus on Organizational Moorings

Organizational moorings anchor us during challenging times. Two specific moorings are described in this section: valuing life-giving organizational purpose and creating mutually shared organizational values. Life-giving purpose and shared values help the community to navigate change.

Valuing Life-Giving Organizational Purpose

Organizational purpose answers the question: why do we exist? A life-giving purpose is one that speaks to our unique existence but also brings hope and energy. Purpose acts like a compass when navigating change. When organizations are going through turbulent storms, times of exponential growth, or stagnation, a life-giving organizational purpose points the way forward and holds people together in the process.

Organizational purpose and organizational goals are often conflated. Stated differently, "purpose is often misunderstood. It is not *what* a group does but *why* it does what it does" (Hill et al. 2014, 92). Goals name what the organization strives to accomplish. Machine organizations often use organizational goals to focus their efforts. But, goals do not address the deeper meaning of why we do what we do.

In organism organizations, leaders are concerned with the health and survival of the organization. Senior leaders often define the organization's purpose and then interact with organizational members as to how the purpose is lived out. Participative leaders ask questions, listen well, and honor the feedback from organizational members. The aggregate feedback they receive informs decisions about how the organizational purpose is lived out and how a planned change initiative could be implemented. Using a power-to mode of operating, senior leaders encourage organizational members to adapt and grow in their role. Planned change aligns with organizational purpose in which leaders and members work together to address the need for change. However, primary control of the organization's purpose and direction is still in the hands of leaders.

In the human brain and energy wave organizations, senior leaders use power-to and power-with practices to foster the development of collaborative organizational purpose. Leaders facilitate discussions where people engage in discovery and articulation of the organizational purpose together. Integrated organizational purpose creates "the strongest possible bond of union" (Follett [1925] 2013, 288). Collaborative leaders want every organizational member to have a sense of belonging and find fulfillment in their work. Shared life-giving organizational purpose provides the focus for the organization to come together. Furthermore, "leaders of the highest type do not conceive their task merely as that of *fulfilling* purpose, but as also that of finding ever larger purposes to fulfil, more fundamental values to be reached" (ibid., 288). In short, "Purpose—not the leader, authority, or power—is what creates and animates a community" (Hill et al. 2014, 92). The iterative changing approach to organizational change thrives in this kind of climate. Life-giving purpose is aspirational and forward looking but it is firmly based in the essence of the organization and why it exists. Life-giving purpose has the capacity to foster employees' ongoing health, development, and fulfillment of their unique purpose. Collaborative actions need to be taken to ensure the continuity and growth of organizational purpose.

The character of leaders will shape the formation of understanding, articulating, and embracing organizational purpose. If leaders operate in a self-protective and selfish manner by coercing employees to comply with their desires with little consideration of the employees' desires, this behavior diminishes employee dignity and depletes energy. Coercion may provoke compliance, but it does not promote commitment to purpose. Whereas if leaders demonstrate trustworthy character and have the good of the employees in mind, this will foster employee dignity and encourage healthy growth. In summary, the mooring of life-giving organizational purpose brings health and fulfillment to an organization, its members, and beyond.

Creating Mutually Shared Organizational Values

Organizational purpose focuses on why we exist, whereas organizational values are "what matters most to us" (Hill et al. 2014, 102). Values are enduring beliefs. Each of us holds values that have been formed throughout our lives. In organizations, we cannot assume that the values we hold will be shared by others.

When leading organizational change, especially collaborative organizational change, it is important that we have honest conversations about what is collectively important to us, our shared values. Leaders need to take time to understand the values of coworkers and clarify shared values that all team members can embrace. Common values help work colleagues to build trust with one another and provide a sense of strength and composure during stormy times. Moreover, "Values characterize what an organization stands for, qualities worthy of esteem or commitment" (Bolman and Deal 2017, 243).

Shared organizational values provide guidance for action. We need shared values to guide our choices about process, to make decisions, to anchor difficult conversations, and to learn together. Shared values shape "priorities and choices, they influence individual and collective thought and action" (Hill et al. 2014, 102). To illustrate, research with leaders of innovation points to four values they all hold in common: "*bold ambition, collaboration, learning*, and *responsibility*" (ibid., 102). These shared values are important to innovative communities. If any one of them was missing, it would be difficult to press forward. These leaders said that in their communities, everyone is responsible for maintaining the "collective identity" (106) that is nurtured by these shared values. Mutual accountability to shared values promotes a healthy working environment.

Organizational moorings of life-giving organizational purpose and mutually shared values promote a sense of belonging, common direction, and sense of fulfillment. Leaders and organizational members who facilitate and inculcate these collaborative moorings provide a sturdy anchor for stormy times and times of change.

Discussion Questions

- Which organization metaphor resonates the most with you? Why?
- Which is your least favorite organization metaphor? Why?
- Tell a story about when you were involved in organizational change. What happened? What did you learn from the experience?
- Think of a time you were in a neutral zone; what helped you make a new beginning?
- In your opinion, what are the signs of healthy organizational change? Unhealthy change?
- How would you describe the relationship between directed change and resistance?
- What are the signs that an organization lacks purpose? What are the benefits of having a strong shared purpose?

The Case of the Growing Non-profit

Dr. Maya leads a non-profit organization named "Thrive" which provides administrative and accounting support services for women-owned small businesses. Since small businesses often don't have money to hire full-time back office support, *Thrive* provides support services so that business owners can focus on growing their companies. Clients can choose from a menu of services for a minimal cost. *Thrive* has a small full-time staff and several part-time specialists. The governing board provides good oversight, has secured numerous grants, and has grown a healthy consistent donor base to provide financial support. *Thrive* is growing steadily and several clients have requested additional services which *Thrive* does not currently offer. Dr. Maya is debating about whether or not they should explore these additional services.

You are a good friend of Dr. Maya's. She has asked you to wrestle with her about the pros and cons of adding new services for clients.

- What are the most important questions for her to consider in evaluating this opportunity?
- How would adding additional client services potentially impact this non-profit?
- What kind of information needs to be gathered to make and support a good decision? With whom should she consult?
- If she decides to investigate the opportunity, what specific questions need to be addressed before approaching her staff, the board, and her clients?
- If consensus is reached about moving forward, how would you suggest that they implement this change in a positive way?
- What are the potential risks or rewards of offering these additional services? What could be some of the unintended consequences?

References

Anderson, Dean, and Linda Ackerman Anderson. 2010. *Beyond Change Management: How to Achieve Breakthrough Results Through Conscious Change Leadership*, 2nd ed. San Francisco: Pfeiffer.

Anderson, Donald L. 2017. *Organization Development: The Process of Leading Organizational Change*. 4th ed. Los Angeles: SAGE.

Argyris, Chris. 1999. *On Organizational Learning*. 2nd ed. Oxford: Wiley-Blackwell.

Avital, Michel. 2008. *Designing Information and Organizations with a Positive Lens, Volume 2*. Edited by Richard J. Boland and David L. Cooperrider. Bingley: Emerald Group Publishing.

Barrett, Frank J., and David L. Cooperrider. 1990. "Generative Metaphor Intervention: A New Approach for Working with Systems Divided by Conflict and Caught in Defensive Perception." *The Journal of Applied Behavioral Science* 26 (2): 219–39. https://doi.org/10.1177/0021886390262011

Bolman, Lee G., and Terrence E. Deal. 2017. *Reframing Organizations: Artistry, Choice, and Leadership.* 6th ed. Hoboken: Wiley.

Bridges, William, and Susan Bridges. 2017. *Managing Transitions: Making the Most of Change.* 25th Anni. ed. Boston: Da Capo Lifelong Books.

Buchanan, David, and Richard Badham. 2008. *Power, Politics, and Organizational Change: Winning the Turf Game.* 2nd ed. Los Angeles: SAGE.

Buono, Anthony F., and Kenneth W. Kerber. 2010. "Creating a Sustainable Approach to Change: Building Organizational Change Capacity." *SAM Advanced Management Journal* 75 (2): 4–21.

Bushe, Gervase R. 1999. "Advances in Appreciative Inquiry as an Organization Development Intervention." *Organization Development Journal* 17 (2): 61–8.

———. 2011. "Appreciative Inquiry: Theory and Critique." In *The Routledge Companion to Organizational Change.* Edited by D. Boje, B. Burnes, and J. Hassard, 88–103. Oxford: Routledge.

Cameron, Kim S. 2008. *Positive Leadership Strategies for Extraordinary Performance.* San Francisco: Berrett-Koehler Publishers.

Colwill, Deborah A. 2009. *Appreciative Leadership.* Paper delivered in Lyon: ISEOR-AOM.

———. 2010. "The Use of Metaphor in Consulting for Organizational Change." In *Consultation for Organizational Change.* Edited by Anthony F. Buono and David W. Jamieson, 113–35. Charlotte: Information Age Publishing.

Cooperrider, David L., and Ronald Fry. 2020. "Appreciative Inquiry in a Pandemic: An Improbable Pairing." *Journal of Applied Behavioral Science* 56 (3): 266–71. https://doi.org/10.1177/0021886320936265

Cooperrider, David L., Diana Whitney, Jacqueline M. Stavros, and Ronald Fry. 2008. *The Appreciative Inquiry Handbook: For Leaders of Change.* 2nd ed. Brunswick: Berrett-Koehler Publishers.

Cummings, Thomas G., and Christopher G. Worley. 2008. *Organization Development and Change.* 9th ed. Mason: Cengage Learning.

Follett, Mary Parker. [1925] 2013. *Dynamic Administration: The Collected Papers of Mary Parker Follett.* Illustrated ed. Mansfield Centre: Martino Fine Books.

Ford, Jeffrey D., and Laurie W. Ford. 2009. "Stop Blaming Resistance to Change and Start Using It." *Organizational Dynamics* 39 (1): 24–36. https://doi.org/10.1016/j.orgdyn.2009.10.002

Hill, Linda A., Greg Brandeau, Emily Truelove, and Kent Lineback. 2014. *Collective Genius: The Art and Practice of Leading Innovation.* Boston: Harvard Business Review Press.

Hughes, Mark. 2016. "Leading Changes: Why Transformation Explanations Fail." *Leadership* 12 (4): 449–69. https://doi.org/10.1177/1742715015571393

———. 2019. *Managing and Leading Organizational Change.* New York: Routledge.

Kerber, Kenneth W., and Anthony F. Buono. 2018. "In Defense of Directed Change: A Viable Approach in the Rhythm of Change." *Academy of Management Annual Meeting Proceedings* 2018 (1): 1–6.

Kotter, John P. [1996] 2012. *Leading Change*. Boston: Harvard Business Review Press.

Kouzes, James M., and Barry Z. Posner. 2016. *Learning Leadership: The Five Fundamentals of Becoming an Exemplary Leader*. Hoboken: Wiley.

Morgan, Gareth. 2006. *Images of Organization*. Updated ed. Thousand Oaks: SAGE.

Pasmore, Bill. 2015. *Leading Continuous Change: Navigating Churn in the Real World*. Oakland: Berrett-Koehler Publishers.

Popova-Nowak, Irina V., and Maria Cseh. 2015. "The Meaning of Organizational Learning: A Meta-Paradigm Perspective." *Human Resource Development Review* 14 (3): 299–331. https://doi.org/10.1177/1534484315596856

Senge, Peter M. [1990] 2006. *The Fifth Discipline: The Art & Practice of The Learning Organization*. Updated ed. New York: Doubleday.

Seo, Myeong-Gu, Linda L. Putnam, and Jean M. Bartunek. 2004. "Dualities and Tensions of Organizational Change." In *Handbook of Organizational Change and Innovation*. Edited by Marshall Scott Poole and Andrew H. Van de Ven, 73–107. Oxford: Oxford University Press.

Sharkey, Linda, Therese F. Yaeger, and Peter F. Sorensen. 2004. "Appreciative Inquiry in a Fortune 50 Global Organization: Extending the AI Concept to Japan." In *Global and International Organization Development*. Edited by Peter F. Sorensen, Thomas C. Head, Therese Yaeger, and David Cooperrider, 517–24. Champaign: Stipes Publishers.

Snow, Charles C. 2015. "Organizing in the Age of Competition, Cooperation, and Collaboration." *Journal of Leadership & Organizational Studies* 22 (4): 433–42. https://doi.org/10.1177/1548051815585852

Spector, Bert. 2013. *Implementing Organizational Change: Theory into Practice*. 3rd ed. Boston: Pearson.

Van de Ven, Andrew H., and Marshall Scott Poole. 1995. "Explaining Development and Change in Organizations." *Academy of Management Review* 20 (3): 510–40. https://doi.org/10.5465/amr.1995.9508080329

Van de Ven, Andrew H., and Kangyong Sun. 2011. "Breakdowns in Implementing Models of Organization Change." *Academy of Management Perspectives* 25 (3): 58–74. https://doi.org/10.5465/amp.25.3.zol58

Worley, Christopher G., Thomas Williams, and Edward E. Lawler III. 2014. *The Agility Factor: Building Adaptable Organizations for Superior Performance*. San Francisco: Jossey-Bass.

Zohar, Danah. 1997. *Rewiring the Corporate Brain*. San Francisco: Berrett-Koehler Publishers.

6 The Triad of Conflict, Power, and Change

Introduction

Chapter 6 brings the triad of conflict, power, and change together. Prior chapters have pointed to the fact that conflict, power, and change are everyday aspects of organizational life. Yet, how they are engaged and experienced differ greatly depending on the context and ethos of the organization. Many settings could be used to illustrate the dynamic interaction of conflict, power, and change. The aim of this chapter is to illustrate the interconnections of conflict, power, and change in two different organizational climates: a controlling climate and a trusting climate. The primary reason for choosing these two climates is to highlight the contrast and emphasize the wide range of possible behaviors and impacts that exist with respect to the confluence of conflict, power, and change in organizations. The two illustrative organizational climates will be unpacked using three arenas of organizational involvement: individual employee capacity, people working together, and the situational pressures of organizational life. In summary, with a view toward understanding the interconnections of conflict, power, and change, three arenas of involvement will be explored within controlling climates and trusting climates.

Arenas of Involvement

Arenas of involvement are the settings of daily activity, participation, and contribution in organizational life. Of the many arenas that could be named, three arenas of involvement described in this chapter include individual employee capacity, people working together, and the situational pressures of organizational life. In order to engage the synthesis of conflict, power,

DOI: 10.4324/9780429323959-6

and change, each of these arenas is explored through two illustrative organizational climates.

Organizational Climate

Whereas organizational culture is a system of shared assumptions, values, and beliefs that govern how people behave in organizations (Schein and Schein 2017), organizational climate is how members experience the culture of an organization in their daily work life. Organizational design and structure influence climate. Climate is experienced at different levels of an organization. For example, the broader organizational climate may be experienced as unsafe whereas team-level interaction might feel psychologically safe; or, vice versa. Leaders play a big part in creating the ethos, atmosphere, and environmental conditions that impact the experience of organizational members. Organizational climate strongly influences employee motivation, engagement, and behavior.

As mentioned previously, the aim of this chapter is to illustrate the synthesis of conflict, power, and change in organizational life. Many types of organizational climates could have been named; however, two contrasting organizational climates have been chosen to highlight the wide range of behaviors and impacts related to the navigation of conflict, power, and change. The two organizational climates that serve as running illustrations throughout the chapter are a controlling climate and a trusting climate.

A controlling climate is one in which managers regularly use coercive tactics with employees to pressure them to comply and perform according to the manager's expectations. When coercion is a primary mode of management, fear is used to bring about the desired result. The push to control employees leads to a culture of distrust and a fear-driven organization (Barrett 2017). If the emphasis on coercive control eclipses other organizational values, then it is likely that managers and employees will exhibit fear-driven behavior. Table 6.1 summarizes the three arenas of involvement in controlling climates.

A trusting climate is one in which leaders create an environment where people feel appreciated and know that their contributions make an impact. Leaders foster employee health and well-being, develop relationships built on mutual trust, and encourage fruitful organizational development and performance. High trust "creates engagement and unleashes creativity, commitment and loyalty" (Barrett 2017, xvi). These dynamics influence the use of conflict, power, and change in the organizational system. Table 6.2 summarizes the three arenas of involvement in trusting climates.

Table 6.1 Three arenas of involvement in controlling climates.

Arena	Manager goals	Manager behaviors	Intended employee outcomes	Unintended consequences	Potential impact on employees
Regulating employee capacity	Employee meets specific objectives and complies with rules	Direction; surveillance; accountability; reward or sanction; power-over tactics; self-promoting or employee empowering behavior	Skilled work; meet objectives; follow rules; compliant behavior	Poor quality work; objectives not met; cover up mistakes; blame others; lack of compliance; frustration with rules; power-from behavior; dysfunction conflict; increased absentee levels; employee turnover	Fear and stress; overly dependent on supervisor direction; decreased personal agency; outgrow prescribed role; disengagement; well-being suffers; dignity violated
Operating smoothly	Work groups meet specific objectives and comply with roles and rules	Direction; surveillance; accountability; minimize conflict; reward or sanction; power-over tactics; self-promoting or employee empowering behavior	Skilled work; meets objectives; smooth work process; transactional roles fulfilled; follow rules; cooperative behavior	Objectives not met; cover up mistakes; blame others; lack of compliance; frustration with roles and rules; power-from behavior; resistance to directed change; power-over behavior; unhealthy competition; dysfunctional conflict; group creativity limited; poor communication	Constrained by prescribed roles; zero-sum mindset grows; mutual mistrust; abrasive or cautious conflict behavior; relationship stress; lack of community and belonging
Reacting to situational pressures	Follow directives; smooth-running operations	Direct change effort; problem solve; create solutions; protect status quo; power-over tactics; self-protective behavior	Follow direction; compliant behavior; quickly restore performance; embed improvements	Solutions may not work; cover up mistakes; solutions mask root issues; resistance to change; power-from behavior; dysfunctional conflict; increased absentee levels; employee turnover	Fear and stress; overworked; change weary; GRASS: guilt, resentment, anxiety, self-absorption, and stress

Table 6.2 Three arenas of involvement in trusting climates.

Arena	Organizational values	Leader priorities	Leader behaviors	Potential impact on employees
Cultivating employee capacity	Human dignity; trustworthy character	Demonstrating care for the well-being of employees; promoting healthy interactions between leaders and employees; supporting the development and performance of employees	Expressing gratitude; encouraging work-life balance; demonstrating trustworthy character; asking questions and listening; promoting experience-driven leadership development; collaborating with employees on performance goals and assessment	Performance decline due to increased learning curve; discovery of latent talents or abilities; increased confidence and competence; meaningful work; high engagement; strong job satisfaction
Collaborating effectively with colleagues	Interpersonal relationships; psychological safety	Developing healthy interpersonal relationships; cultivating strong team dynamics	Building mutual trust and respect among team members; fostering power-with mindset and practices; stewarding productive task conflict; nurturing psychological safety; encouraging diverse voices; giving and receiving feedback	Supported, cared for, and valued; learning and growth occur; productive conflict capability; agency and power-with practices; uncomfortable conversations; possibility of manipulation; creativity, energy, and teamwork
Responding to situational pressures	Life-giving purpose; mutually shared values	Deepening the culture of trust; using the situational pressures to grow and learn	Focusing on shared purpose and values; generating coactive framing of the situation; growing in collaborative change capacity	Change weary; chaos and confusion; fulfillment of personal purpose; willingness to contribute; experience mutual support

Arena One: Individual Employee Capacity

The first arena of involvement is individual employee capacity. This arena involves the participation, contribution, and development of employees as they engage the organizational road. As mentioned earlier, organizational climate is how members experience the culture of an organization, department, or team in their daily work life. Organizational climate strongly influences employee motivation, engagement, and behavior. We will explore individual employee capacity in controlling climates and trusting climates.

Regulating Employee Capacity in Controlling Climates

Attempting to control the behavior of employees can happen in any type of system and at any level of an organization. However, some organizational structures are more disposed to controlling employee behaviors than others. For example, in mechanistic organizations, hierarchical position power provides a platform to exercise control. Mintzberg (1983, 144) states in bureaucratic systems, "impersonal standards are established that guide the behavior of employees." These standards control the content of work through rules, policies, procedures, and job descriptions (ibid., 144). Standards regulate employee output or performance through "control systems" (144). Standards also formalize "the skills and knowledge" needed for the work through "training and selection" of employees (144). In short, leaders of bureaucratic organizations prescribe and set expectations of employee roles, rules, and behaviors.

Managers ensure that employees meet specific work objectives and comply with the rules. To accomplish this, manager behaviors include directing employees in their work, surveilling the work, and holding employees accountable for their work. Managers have the ability to reward or sanction employees' behavior as well as use other power tactics to ensure employees comply. Direction and surveillance of employees' work product and performance take time and energy. Holding employees accountable through pragmatic power-over mode is the easiest way to accomplish outcomes but not the best way in the long run (Follett [1925] 2013). In other words, "Coercion works along the lines of behavior modification. It has, as a result a limited impact since it is task-oriented and the continual deployment of either the carrot or stick may be necessary to ensure the desired behavior is sustained" (Hardy 1996, S7). Coercive management behavior may be fueled by "Theory X" assumptions that employees dislike work, avoid responsibility, and need to be directed and controlled (McGregor [1960] 2006).

A "fear-based" system inculcates "stress-inducing values such as control, manipulation, hierarchy, and status seeking" (Barrett 2017, xxi). Status seeking managers may use a variety of self-promoting behaviors to safeguard or advance their own position in the organization. This fear-driven energy is channeled toward selfish competitive purposes. For example, managers who want to demonstrate their ability to exceed their departmental quotas may take advantage of employees by applying heavy pressure on them to beat deadlines, improve work quality, and increase productivity. Schein and Schein (2018, 106) observe "self-centered abuse of power is never successful in the long run, despite individualized reward systems that favor selfishness over selflessness."

On the other hand, managers in bureaucratic systems who are not as motivated by status seeking self-promoting outcomes and who choose to put priority on the needs of employees will likely demonstrate employee empowering behaviors. Even though the broader organizational climate may be overtly controlling, these managers create a sense of calm, safety, and mutual loyalty in their local part of the organizational system. In other words, these humble leaders seek to foster a climate with their direct reports where employees feel valued and respected (Schein and Schein 2018). These managers may be motivated by "Theory Y" assumptions that employees have a natural desire to work, will work toward goals to which they are committed, and will seek out and accept responsibility (McGregor [1960] 2006). These managers see their role not to coerce and control employees but to create opportunities where both the employees and the organization will benefit. However, in real-life scenarios, these above-described on-the-road behaviors might be used for the good of all concerned; for self-advancing purposes; or perhaps a tacit blend of both.

In bureaucratic systems, managers are expected to drive employees toward intended outcomes. Basic employee outcomes could include delivering skilled work on time, meeting work objectives, following the rules, and complying with their manager's wishes. Despite the fact that managers prescribe intended employee outcomes, employees may deliver poor quality work or not meet their objectives. In a fear-driven controlling climate, employees may try to cover up mistakes or blame others in order to deflect the consequences.

If employee outcomes are not met, managers may use power-over tactics to enforce compliance in order to accomplish results. However, manager tactics used to coerce employee behavior may lead to unintended consequences such as deliberate lack of compliance, visible frustration with rules or expectations, dysfunctional conflict, increased absentee levels, and employee turnover. Coercive behaviors harm those who are targets of these tactics. Being subject to sustained power-over behavior may give rise to simmering resentment, subtle sabotage, or power-from behaviors. In short, coercive management behavior "may engender a backlash in the people over whom power is exercised" (Hardy 1996, S7).

Controlling climates will have other impacts on employees. The emphasis on coercive control by managers may arouse fear and stress in employees who wonder if they will be able to accomplish their work and measure up to the standards of their boss. To curb fear, some employees may choose to become overly dependent on their supervisor for direction which stunts their growth and decreases their personal agency. Many employees will outgrow their prescribed roles, which may lead to boredom, reduced motivation, and eventually disengagement. Ironically, employees may be both overworked and underchallenged.

A culture of fear and distrust "inhibits self-expression, openness and transparency, and creates disengagement" (Barrett 2017, xvi). Moreover, "Negative power is merely power applied to constrain and dominate others. It limits rather than expands human talent" (Fairholm 2009, xxviii). For instance, when leaders belittle or micromanage employee efforts, the effects of these actions deplete the soul and drain energy. Left unchecked, these power-over tactics have damaging effects on people. Diminishing someone's potential is demeaning and will decrease their capacity. In unsafe controlling climates, employee well-being suffers and dignity is violated (Hicks 2019). Barrett (2017, 25) observes "a climate of stress and fear; hierarchical structures of control; bureaucratic procedures; and authoritarian managers who control, micro-manage and manipulate their staff" lead to a "disengaged work force." Coercive manager behavior decreases employee capacity.

Cultivating Employee Capacity in Trusting Climates

Human beings have potential for growth. Leaders who foster trusting organizational climates recognize "the distinctive potential contribution of the human being . . . *at every level of the organization*" (McGregor [1960] 2006, 154). This contribution stems from the individual's "capacity to think, to plan, to exercise judgment, to be creative, to direct and control" their own behavior (ibid., 154). Recognizing, encouraging, and cultivating individual capacity of organizational members is a central concern in high trust systems because leaders desire to see members flourish (Barrett 2017). In trusting climates, leaders pursue priorities that support and cultivate individual employee capacity. The priorities could include demonstrating care for the well-being of employees, promoting healthy interactions between leaders and employees, and supporting the development and performance of employees.

Demonstrating Care for the well-being of Employees

In trusting climates, demonstrating care for employee well-being is an important priority. Two specific behaviors that demonstrate care for employees are expressing gratitude and encouraging work-life balance.

Expressing gratitude involves paying attention to the hard work and unique contributions that employees make, recognizing how these contributions are beneficial to the team and organization, and deliberately expressing appreciation to employees about these contributions. Expressions of gratitude may strengthen employees' confidence and encourage their growth. Spreitzer (2006, 308) observes "when individuals become aware of their strengths, they recognize more of their full potential." Expressing gratitude honors the dignity of an employee and may foster a sense of belonging and welcome. Tangible expressions of genuine appreciation such as handwritten notes are particularly meaningful. Chapter 4 discusses the organizational mooring of valuing human dignity as essential to healthy organizations.

Leaders demonstrate care for employee well-being by modeling and encouraging work-life balance. Work-life balance refers to the prioritization of time and energy that is devoted to work, family, self-care, and other commitments. Time management, learning to say "no," and getting enough sleep are examples of well-being behaviors that support work-life balance. When leaders model work-life balance, it opens the door for employees to do the same. Leaders need to actively encourage hardworking employees to care for their health, take breaks, and enjoy vacation time so that they stay healthy and refreshed. Watching for signs of employee burnout or disengagement should be on a leader's radar as well.

Promoting Healthy Interactions Between Leaders and Employees

In cultivating individual capacity, a second priority is promoting healthy interactions between leaders and employees. Essential leader behaviors that promote this priority are demonstrating trustworthy character and asking generative questions and listening well.

Trust is central to healthy relationships. Trustworthy leader character sets the tone for relationships with coworkers and creates environments where healthy interactions can thrive. Leaders demonstrate trustworthy behavior by respecting coworkers, speaking with honesty and compassion, keeping their promises, and honoring their commitments. They are both credible and competent. They deliberately nurture trust in daily life and "demonstrate that they care about their people and the common good" (Barrett 2017, xxiii). For collaborative power to flourish in a system, mutual trust is needed among leaders and members. Chapter 4 describes the organizational mooring of valuing trustworthy character.

Leaders do a lot of telling; however, if they desire to encourage healthy interactions with employees, they need to ask generative questions and listen well. Question posing is an artform in which you draw out the ideas and reflections of others. Most people can discern whether or not a question is asked with authentic interest and genuine curiosity. Leaders need to ask thought-provoking questions that engage the world of the employee and then listen intently to the interests and concerns raised. Listening requires deliberate focused attention on what another is saying, discipline to remain quiet while another is speaking, and asking follow-up questions that draw out the full meaning of the other person (Colwill 2005). If leaders have a humble learning posture, then this provides a safe fertile ground for employees to openly share honest insights and dissenting opinions. Deep listening conveys respect; the person's dignity is valued and honored when they feel safe and heard (Hicks 2019). Kouzes and Posner (2016, 90) state, "to become the best leader you can be, you have to know deep down what *others* want and need. You have to understand *their* hopes, *their* dreams, *their* needs, and *their* interests." Chapter 3 explores listening and respecting as a basis for generative dialogue.

Supporting the Development and Performance of Employees

Leaders who foster trusting climates seek to facilitate whole-person growth. In the arena of cultivating individual employee capacity, a third priority is supporting the development and performance of employees. Aligning with this priority are two possible leader behaviors: promoting experience-driven leadership development and collaborating with employees regarding their own performance goals and assessment.

Organizational leaders have the opportunity to promote experience-driven leadership development with employees. Leadership development can occur throughout high trust systems, since leaders "exist in all corners and levels of all organizations" (Schein and Schein 2018, xi). Developing leadership competence is best learned through intentional on-the-ground experience (McCauley et al. 2013). Unlike high-control systems that restrict employees to assigned prescribed roles, high trust systems encourage intentional cross-training and variety of experience. Increasing the variety of experience is particularly important to stretch and strengthen employees' existing skills and to promote discovery of latent abilities or gifts. One way to increase variety of experience is through "development-in-place" opportunities (ibid., 21). Development-in-place opportunities could include taking on unfamiliar responsibilities, exploring new directions, increasing one's scope and scale of responsibility, attempting to influence without authority, or working across cultures (22). Other examples include shadowing senior leaders or interacting with role models (DeRue and Workman 2013). In developing employee leadership competence, it is crucial to identify appropriate experience-based challenges and locate where employees can exercise these experiences (McCauley et al. 2013, 23). Three possible strategic locations for development-in-place assignments are "reshaping the job, taking on temporary assignments, and seeking challenges outside the workplace" (ibid., 23). Throughout the development-in-place process, employees will benefit from asking others for ideas and feedback (23). Experience, practice, and reflection on experience are key to ongoing growth.

Collaborating with employees regarding their own performance goals and assessment is another important leader behavior. As mentioned earlier, promoting regular healthy interactions with employees forms the basis of trust. During these trust-filled interactions, leaders can intentionally mentor employees. Through regular mentoring conversations, leaders cultivate power-to opportunities for employees to grow in their own self-assessment regarding their development and performance. In other words, leaders can encourage employees to grow in their own agency, empowerment, and development. Employees need to see themselves as valued whole persons (Schein and Schein 2018). The power-to practices that leaders exercise create space for employee growth. Quinn and Spreitzer (1997, 41) state "Empowerment, then, is not something that management does to employees, but rather a mind-set that employees have about their role in the organization. While management can create a context that is more empowering, employees must choose to be empowered." Empowered people deliberately and freely perform their work, their work is important to them, they have competence and confidence to do their work, and they believe their work will contribute and have impact (ibid., 41). Leaders need to provide encouragement, reduce the barriers that block empowerment, and trust that employees will be responsible in their agency (43). The primary aim is for employees to "identify, develop, and leverage their unique strengths and talents" (Spreitzer 2006, 307). Leveraging strength does not mean ignoring weakness (ibid., 308). However, "when leaders help others to identify and nurture their strengths, they build awareness of possibilities, generate hope about the future, and encourage others to take courageous action to become their hoped-for possible selves" (308).

In summary, leaders cultivate individual employee capacity by demonstrating care for their well-being, promoting healthy interactions, and supporting employee development and performance. Many potential impacts could result from these initiatives. For example, with the focus on stretching, growing, and trying new experiences, one possible impact is that employee work performance may decline due to increased learning curve. When people are learning new behaviors, it takes time and energy to achieve competence and mastery. Leaders need to be aware that employee performance may decline temporarily when people are learning new skills or acclimating to a new challenge. On the other hand, employees may grow in competence or discover latent talents or abilities when engaged in challenging new assignments. Another impact could be increased confidence of employees when they are genuinely recognized and rewarded for doing good work. Leaders cultivate trusting climates in which employees experience meaningful work, high engagement, and strong job satisfaction. And, "meaningful work is vital to full engagement" (Kouzes and Posner 2016, 93).

Arena Two: People Working Together

A second arena of involvement in daily organizational life is people working together. We spend many hours of our life interacting with people in our work environments. The people we work with and our relationships with these individuals have a significant impact on us. Interaction among coworkers is necessary to accomplish the work. Yet, how people interact may differ greatly depending on the context and ethos of the organization. We will look at the arena of people working together in controlling climates and trusting climates.

Operating Smoothly in Controlling Climates

In controlling climates, managers emphasize the importance of people working together in a seamless fashion. Managers expect work groups to fulfill specific objectives which could include producing skilled work, delivering work product on time, executing smooth running operations, and demonstrating cooperative behavior. In addition, work groups need to fulfill their assigned transactional roles, and follow the rules, policies, and procedures.

Managers focus on ensuring work groups comply with directives and meet objectives. To accomplish this, manager behaviors include direction, surveillance, and accountability of work group performance and product. Managers also seek to minimize work group conflict so as to keep operations moving smoothly. In controlling climates, managers will use rewards and sanctions to motivate or coerce work groups to accomplish their work. Power-over tactics may be more heavily used by managers if their positional authority is not respected or followed by work group members. Chapter 4 describes some common power-over tactics. As mentioned previously, depending upon their personal values, managers may coercively drive work group performance for their own self-promoting status seeking purposes; or, managers may demonstrate employee empowering behavior to care for the needs of employees, the work group, and the organization. Additionally, the personal values and behaviors that managers exhibit will spread to coworkers. For example, if self-promoting behavior is demonstrated by managers, then employees learn this is an accepted way of operating and may try to follow the example. Whereas if managers exhibit humble leader behaviors, this encourages coworkers to engage with dignity and follow this example (Schein and Schein 2018).

Unintended consequences in a controlling climate could include poor quality work product or unmet work group objectives. In a fear-driven system, work groups may attempt to cover up mistakes, blame each other, or blame another part of the organizational system for the errors. Interpersonal conflict may ensue over who is at fault. Additional unintended consequences could include lack of compliance with their supervisor's wishes, frustration with prescribed roles and rules, and resistance to directed change. Likewise, a variety of power-from behaviors may be exhibited in opposition or retaliation to the highly controlled environment or to coercive manager behavior.

A controlling climate impacts both employees and their work groups. When people are assigned prescribed roles within work groups, they may feel constricted or underchallenged. As such, desire for promotion or important work group roles may foster zero-sum competition among members. Or, if rewards are given to only a few high-performing individuals in the work group, this may fuel self-promoting behavior. Resentment may build up within group members which decreases motivation to work together. When group members are under stress and in competition with one another, their interpersonal conflicts may become overly abrasive or accommodating or avoidant depending on their default conflict styles. Internally, work group members may exhibit power-over tactics with one another driving unhealthy competition, dysfunctional conflict, and a "survival of the fittest" mentality. The resulting damage to coworker relationships may cause anxiety and stress. Unhealthy relational conflict erodes trust among team members and breaks down their ability to communicate. Group creativity is limited when people do not feel safe to share new ideas or dissenting opinions. Time and energy are wasted in unhealthy competition or dysfunctional conflict that could be spent in more constructive ways. In short, power-over competition and conflict among coworkers will disrupt their ability to seamlessly work together and can reduce productivity levels. Singh (2009, 166) observes, "When a person seeks not merely power, but control as well, conflicts tend to increase." A "fear-based" culture will "create separation and mistrust and decrease well-being" (Barrett 2017, 18). As a result, there is a lack of community and belonging; the fear-based work group may become "life depleting and disconnecting" (ibid., 18).

Collaborating Effectively With Colleagues in Trusting Climates

Barrett (2017, 70) states, "A basic need for all organizations is to create harmonious interpersonal relationships and good internal communication."

Therefore, leaders who seek to foster trusting climates will focus on collaborating effectively with colleagues. Two priorities that support collaborating effectively with colleagues include developing healthy interpersonal relationships and cultivating strong team dynamics.

Developing Healthy Interpersonal Relationships

Many behaviors promote the priority of developing healthy interpersonal relationships. Two behaviors are noted here: building mutual trust and respect among team members and fostering power-with mindset and practices.

As mentioned previously, leaders with trustworthy character nurture a safe climate to cultivate individual employee capacity. Additionally, these leaders can foster mutual trust and respect among team members to promote healthy relationships. Kouzes and Posner (2016, 163) assert "trust building involves creating an environment in which people can be open and honest with each other." These positive relationships are characterized by "a true sense of mutuality and relatedness, such that people experience mutual giving and receiving, caring, and safety in challenging times" (DeRue and Workman 2013, 792). Positive relationships are nurtured by expressing "compassion, trust, respect, and gratitude" (Spreitzer 2006, 313). Creating and maintaining trusting interpersonal relationships "require a learning mindset, cooperative attitudes, and skills in interpersonal and group dynamics" (Schein and Schein 2018, 20). In healthy collaborative relationships, each party is committed to the interests of their colleagues as much as they are to their own interests, "this commitment reduces the need for the continual assessment of trust" (Snow 2015, 435). The relationship itself is highly valued; as a result, there is mutual trust and confidence that the rewards and recognition for excellent team work will be equitably allocated (ibid., 435). In other words, power-over tactics, unhealthy competition, and dysfunctional conflict are reduced in high trust climates. In short, building mutual trust and respect will help employees develop healthy relationships in their organizations. Kouzes and Posner (2017, 18) observe "The more people trust their leaders, and each other, the more they take risks, make changes, and keep moving ahead." Chapter 3 explores the organizational mooring of valuing interpersonal relationships.

In trusting climates, leaders develop healthy relationships among colleagues by fostering power-with mindset and practices. As discussed in Chapter 4, the use of power in organizations often stems from a power-over mindset. Power-over tactics are generally thought to be "coercive," whereas power-with mindset and practices are "coactive" (Follett 1924). Coactive simply means that people freely collaborate together to create something new. In other words, organizational leaders and members work together with common purpose to achieve mutually shared life-giving outcomes. Leaders need to encourage coactive power capacity across the organization. Power-with mindset and practices are experientially learned. As colleagues work together, they grow in understanding how their roles and behaviors impact each other in seeking to accomplish their shared goals. Komives and Wagner (2017, 25) observe, "Collaboration implies mutually beneficial goals, engaged participants, shared responsibility, and self-aware individuals." Follett (1924) believed power-with capacity needs continual developing, whereas power-over tactics need diminishing. She adds, "One way of reducing power-over is through integration" (Follett [1925] 2013, 104). Integration is a way of engaging conflict so that the desires of both parties are represented, a creative solution is crafted, and "neither side has had to sacrifice anything" (ibid., 32). Integrating coworkers' interests frees the parties from being stuck "within the boundaries of two alternatives which are mutually exclusive" and reframes the win-lose conflict toward inventing an option that fully encompasses both parties' desires (33). For example, Hill et al. (2014, 192) advocate for the practice of "creative resolution" which is "the ability to make integrative decisions that combine disparate or even opposing ideas." In practicing creative resolution, "leaders create the space for integration by keeping things simple, flexible, and open" (ibid., 186). Chapter 4 describes additional power-with practices and their benefit to organizations.

Cultivating Strong Team Dynamics

In addition to developing healthy interpersonal relationships, another central priority is cultivating strong team dynamics. A wide variety of behaviors could support this priority. Four interconnected behaviors are explored in this section: stewarding productive task conflict, nurturing psychological safety, encouraging diverse voices, and giving and receiving feedback.

In high trust climates, cultivating strong team dynamics is necessary for daily life on the organizational road. One behavior that is crucial to strong team dynamics is stewarding productive task conflict. Broadly speaking, stewards are entrusted with responsibility to appropriately handle resources for the benefit of others. Productive task conflict is a resource that is entrusted to a team to steward for the benefit of the individual team members, the team, and the organization. In other words, when teams engage in conflict, they seek not only their own interests but also the interests of others. Stewarding healthy productive conflict has the capacity to deepen relationships, promote collaboration, enhance performance, improve decision-making, and stimulate innovation. Rather than seeing conflict as something to be avoided, leaders and members can routinely create a calm space so that substantive difference of opinion can be voiced and generative dialogue promoted. By cultivating substantive conversations, leaders can strengthen the confidence of team members in their ability to engage productive task conflict toward generative results. In addition, dealing wisely with relational conflict is important since heated relational conflict is associated with negative impacts on team collaboration capacity (Raines 2020). Colleagues can help one another grow in awareness of the team's conflict patterns and the personal default conflict styles of individual members. Reflection on these insights can promote growth for both teams and individuals. Learning how to productively steward conflict is a group capacity that brings great benefit to high trust systems. The process of integration transforms conflict into an opportunity to create a new collaborative whole (Follett 1924). In trusting climates, organizational members and leaders steward productive task conflict so that it serves the purposes of the individuals, the group, and the organization. Chapter 3 explores generative dialogue and healthy organizational conflict in more depth.

For task conflict to be productive, leaders need to nurture psychological safety among colleagues. Psychological safety describes a climate where people feel comfortable expressing themselves, even if their opinion is a dissenting one (Edmondson 2019). According to the research of Hicks (2019, 85), "Across all settings, the element of dignity that was violated the most was safety." In an unsafe climate, stress levels increase and daily work becomes more difficult to accomplish. Learning and innovation are stifled in an unsafe environment. Teamwork and interpersonal relationships deteriorate when psychological safety is lacking. Therefore, creating and reinforcing an environment of safety, trust, and collaboration is necessary to support strong team dynamics. Leaders create the conditions for psychological safety, however it is "a property of a group" (Edmondson 2019, 8). Experimenting and learning are enhanced in a climate of psychological safety. Chapter 3 explores the organizational mooring of valuing psychological safety.

Within a trusting climate of psychological safety, another important behavior is encouraging diverse voices to speak. Authentic voicing is supported by the dialogue practices of listening, respecting, and suspending judgment (Isaacs 1999). Drawing out differing perspectives invites "intellectual diversity" (Hill et al. 2014, 139). The team needs to engage "whoever has pertinent information or expertise to speak up and improve whatever the group is seeking to accomplish" (Schein and Schein 2018, 20). Diverse viewpoints are needed for productive task conflict and collaborative innovation to flourish. Komives and Wagner (2017, 25) observe "Collaboration means learning to nurture relationships in which influence and good ideas come inclusively from all directions. Collaborative groups benefit from these diverse perspectives." Hill et al. (2014, 117) assert "the primary role of the leader is to create an environment where diversity and creative conflict flourish, experimentation is encouraged, intelligent missteps tolerated and integrative decision making embraced." Encouraging diverse voices to speak fosters power-to engagement with the goal of power-with collaboration and innovation. To encourage diverse voices to speak out, leaders need to bring teams together in creating shared rules of engagement, or ground rules for discussion. The rules are coactively built and everyone agrees to mutually hold each other accountable.

In trusting climates, giving and receiving feedback is crucial to cultivating strong team dynamics. Leaders need to model giving and receiving feedback if they desire to grow this capacity in a team or organization. In general, leaders need to clearly articulate that "the purpose of feedback is to promote a learning environment for everyone in the organization" (Hicks 2019, 89). High trust systems value feedback and make it a routine part of ongoing interactions. Everyone can participate in this power-with practice. However, giving and receiving feedback may be difficult in the beginning because of "built-in resistance" to it and "there will most likely be a growth curve in everyone's ability to feel comfortable" with the process (ibid., 89). Even though the process may be messy and uncomfortable at first, over time leaders and members can grow in their competence and discernment about giving and receiving feedback.

In summary, the arena of collaborating effectively with colleagues focuses on developing healthy interpersonal relationships and cultivating strong team dynamics which provides fertile soil for growth. Employees feel supported, cared for, valued, and have a sense of belonging (Barrett 2017). As agency and power-with practices increase, uncomfortable and messy conversations will happen. But as people give and receive honest gracious feedback to one another, both teams and individuals will learn and grow. Leaders need to steward their power toward growing coactive power, and not use power as an opportunity to selfishly manipulate others. If leaders actively encourage collaborating effectively with colleagues, then creativity, energy, and teamwork are unleashed toward rigorous and innovative results.

Arena Three: Situational Pressures of Organizational Life

A third arena of involvement is attuning to the situational pressures of an organization. Life on the organizational road can be hectic and messy. Organizational members and leaders must pay attention to and address the pressure points. All organizations confront some common pressures: negotiating priorities, making time sensitive decisions, delivering product or service on schedule, or adapting under external pressure. However, the multifaceted nature of situational pressures will take different forms depending on the unique factors within an organization. We will explore the third arena of situational pressures in controlling climates and trusting climates.

Reacting to Situational Pressures in Controlling Climates

Reacting to situational pressures may be challenging in organizations where high control is valued and uncertainty is mitigated. When high-control systems experience situational pressures, managers will react differently depending on what happens. If the situational pressure does not substantively impact the performance of the organization, then managers may or may not intervene. But, if an urgent situational pressure occurs that greatly impacts performance, managers will react with a directed change approach to restore system equilibrium. In this second case, management goals for employees are to follow directives and cooperate in restoring smooth-running operations.

In an urgent situation, the primary management behavior is to direct the change event in order to solve the problem and restore performance. The goal is to identify the problem, analyze the cause, evaluate possible solutions, and develop action plans to implement the solution (Cooperrider et al. 2008). A malfunctioning system costs the organization time and money. Therefore, tremendous pressure is put on organizational managers and members to fix the problem that is causing their system to slow down or stop. In controlling climates, managers act to solve the immediate problem, but also seek to protect the status quo and restore equilibrium. The uncertainty of an unresolved problem may fuel managers' use of power-over tactics to fix the issue. In other words, managers often use a strategy of "telling" to lead change and if that doesn't work they use a "forcing" strategy (Quinn 2000, 10). During a time of high stress, self-protective manager behavior may also increase due to the urgency and high visibility of the pressure point.

In controlling climates, if situational pressures are substantive and urgent, managers want employees to follow direction, demonstrate compliant behavior, and quickly restore performance by implementing the solutions. However, one unintended consequence could be that the implemented solutions don't work. A variety of reasons could contribute to a failed change effort. For example, under pressure, managers may prematurely jump to conclusions and make poor decisions on how to solve the problem based on weak assessment of the situation, not gathering enough information, and not seeking valuable input from coworkers. Without a more complete understanding of what is occurring in the organizational system, it is difficult to diagnose a situation correctly. Another reason might be that organizational members may oppose the change and "sabotage" the effort (Bridges and Bridges 2017). Additionally, managers and employees may try to cover up mistakes that are made or engage in dysfunctional conflict to assign blame for what happened. A failed change effort increases anxiety and mistrust in an organization. Since the problem still exists, the directed change approach is once again applied with even more pressure until the issue is resolved. Quinn (2000, 11) states "The forcing strategy usually evokes anger, resistance, and damage to the fundamental relationship" and this forcing strategy "is not likely to result in the kind of voluntary commitment that is necessary to sustain the system." Another possible scenario is that the solutions and improvements that were implemented temporarily fix the problem, but only in the short term. The unintended consequence is that the solution is merely a stopgap fix which masks the root issues. In other words, the symptoms were addressed but not the root issue itself. The underlying problem will likely resurface again.

When high-control systems add increased pressure on employees to quickly solve substantive problems, fear and stress levels go up. During an emergency, employees may be pressured to work overtime and become fatigued due to overwork. In this environment, people can easily become weary of the directed change effort. A high stress environment could lead to increased absentee levels and employee turnover. Managers may fail to account for the psychological impact of the transitions that employees are facing during organizational change (Bridges and Bridges 2017). There are tangible costs of not managing employee transition effectively. Five lingering costs are "guilt, resentment, anxiety, self-absorption, and stress" (ibid., 153). The long-term effect of these lingering costs will impact employees' well-being and their ability to contribute to the organization. Chapter 5 discusses managing transitions in more depth.

Fear-driven cultures focus on "self-interest" (Barrett 2017, xvii). As a result, managers may not pay attention to the impact that high-control systems have on employees. Bolman and Deal (2017, 356) state "Many views of leadership fail to recognize its relational and contextual nature." In controlling climates, the driving values of efficiency, productivity, and control may overpower the relational and contextual nature of leadership. Even if leaders attempt to focus on protecting employee needs, the organizational design of bureaucratic structures pushes toward positional authority, control, and power-over task-orientation.

Responding to Situational Pressures in Trusting Climates

All organizations face situational pressures. As described earlier, high-control systems use hierarchical structure and task-orientation to manage operations and assess quality. Noted in Chapter 5, this type of system has difficulty adapting to environmental pressures. By contrast, high trust systems cultivate positive relationships and collaborative team dynamics to achieve organizational goals. Mutual trust rather than directed control is the element that holds this type of system together during difficult times. In responding to situational pressures, leaders who foster a trusting climate have at least two overarching priorities: deepening the culture of trust and using situational pressures to learn and grow.

Deepening the Culture of Trust

Deepening the culture of trust is an important priority when responding to situational pressures. In describing organizational culture, it is helpful "to think of culture as what the group has learned in its efforts to survive, grow, deal with its external environment, and organize itself" (Schein and Schein 2017, 14). Thus, organizational culture forms and deepens during times of stress and pressure. Leaders need to help the organization effectively navigate situational pressures, but also recognize that these pressures are an opportunity to strengthen the culture of trust. In other words, "leadership and culture formation are two sides of the same coin" (ibid., xiv). In response to situational pressures, two broad leader behaviors that cultivate and deepen a high trust culture are focusing on shared purpose and values and encouraging coactive framing of the situation.

Focusing on shared purpose and values is a leader behavior that cultivates and deepens a culture of trust. When organizations face situational pressures, people may feel stress, anxiety, or fear. Formal and informal leaders can lessen the anxiety in the system by reminding people of their shared purpose and values which bring a sense of stability to an uncertain time. Purpose focuses on why we exist, whereas values are "what matters most to us" (Hill et al. 2014, 102).

Organizational purpose acts like a compass when navigating change or facing situational pressures. A life-giving organizational purpose brings people together and gives them a common focal point. When facing situational pressures, shared purpose guides the way forward and builds coworker camaraderie in the process. Collaboration is enhanced with a shared common purpose. In high trust systems, leaders want every organizational member to have a sense of belonging and find fulfillment in their work. Purpose "is what creates and animates a community" (Hill et al. 2014, 92). Life-giving purpose is hopeful and forward looking but it is firmly based in the essence of the organization and why it exists. High trust systems coactively ensure the continuity and growth of organizational purpose.

Organizational values describe shared commitments; they are the moorings that anchor us during stormy times. Bolman and Deal (2017, 243) state "Values characterize what an organization stands for, qualities worthy of esteem or commitment." Shared values serve to guide, direct, and protect through focusing us on what is important. Mutual accountability to shared values promotes a healthy working environment. Shared values shape "priorities and choices, they influence individual and collective thought and action" (Hill et al. 2014, 102). During stressful times, common values provide a sense of strength and composure. Collaboratively working through stressful situations can deepen mutual trust among colleagues. When responding to situational pressures, shared values and mutual trust support collegial behavior. Clear organizational values provide guidance and stability when quick action needs to take place.

Shared organizational purpose and values create a sense of community and inspire collaborative interaction. However, if leaders use the naming of organizational purpose and values to selfishly manipulate coworkers into complying with something that is not in the best interest of their coworkers, then inspirational appeals toward purpose and values have deteriorated into coercion. In contrast, when organizational purpose and values are mutually shared and foster the common good, then well-being and genuine collaborative work can flourish. Chapter 5 describes the organizational moorings of life-giving organizational purpose, mutually shared organizational values, and their importance in navigating organizational change.

To deepen a culture of trust when facing situational pressures, a second helpful leader behavior is generating coactive framing of the situation. Simply stated "Framing refers to the ways in which facts or perceptions are defined, constructed, or labeled" (Raines 2020, 59). Schon (1987, 4) observes, "Depending on our disciplinary backgrounds, organizational roles, past histories, interests, and political/economic perspectives, we frame problematic situations in different ways." Thus, when situational pressures arise, how they are framed depends on who is framing them. Each person has the opportunity to frame the situational pressure from their perspective. Due to their platform, organizational leaders often have more agency in framing the situation. Yet, in high trust cultures leaders have the opportunity to generate coactive framing power by asking honest questions and attentively listening to how coworkers uniquely frame the situational pressure from their vantage points. Divergent perspectives that articulate unique expertise, experience, and background bring vital fresh insights and information which can benefit the discussion. The wisdom gained from openly collaborating together on the organizational balcony is invaluable and creative alternatives for handling the situational pressure can be explored. By contrast, leaders can selfishly use the power of framing to manipulate employee behavior.

Coercive framing that shows little consideration of the employees' desires and opinions diminishes employee dignity and depletes energy. Coercion may provoke compliance, but it does not promote commitment. Instead, coactive framing involves doing the hard work of building mutual trust and operating with honesty, transparency, and integrity. Trust must be cultivated, "it cannot be bought or commanded, inherited or enforced. To maintain it, leaders must continually earn it" (DePree 2003, 124). If leaders generate coactive framing of situational pressures, then this will deepen the culture of trust, foster employee dignity, and encourage healthy growth.

Using Situational Pressures to Learn and Grow

In trusting climates, when situational pressures appear, a second broad priority is using the situational pressures to grow and learn. A leader behavior that supports this priority is growing in collaborative change capacity. When situational pressures occur in high trust systems, people collaboratively engage in bringing about change. The pressure point is an opportunity to regenerate and bring new life to the system. Therefore, situational pressures provide the opportunity for leaders to foster collaborative change capacity. Buono and Kerber (2010, 4) state "change capacity is the ability of an organization to change not just once, but as a normal response to changes in its environment."

By contrast, when situational pressures arise in controlling climates, the goal is to solve the problem and restore performance. This type of change model is linear and sequential, with a heavy reliance on the top leader to direct the change effort. A leader-centered model of change is overrated (Hughes 2019). Schein and Schein (2018, 6) state, "it is virtually impossible for an individual to accumulate enough knowledge to figure out all of the answers. Interdependence and constant change become a way of life in which humility in the face of this complexity has become a critical survival skill."

In trusting climates, leaders strive for interdependence and shape the context in which others are willing and able to participate. Collaborative change capacity is coactive, fluid, and regenerative. It entails responding to situational pressures by flipping the problem or issue into an opportunity for growth (Cooperrider et al. 2008). Collaborative change capacity requires coactive power-with mindset and supporting behaviors. When power is used for good, it attracts energy, life, and health. Trusting relationships promote psychological safety needed to creatively turn obstacles into opportunities to learn, grow, and regenerate. Both leaders and members are collaborators in the unfolding of ongoing change. This fluid approach to change can be effective in organizations that require learning and innovation as their mainstay (Colwill 2010). Moreover, "this approach attempts to take full advantage of the expertise and creativity of organizational members, reconfiguring existing practices and models and testing new ideas and perspectives" (Buono and Kerber 2010, 8). Learning to experiment is a prime example of growing in collaborative change capacity. Collaborative teams can use the situational pressure to "Pursue new ideas quickly and proactively through multiple experiments"; "Reflect on and analyze the outcomes of their experiments"; and "Adjust subsequent actions and choices based on what they've learned" (Hill et al. 2014, 163). These experimenting phases are "iterative and recursive" in nature (ibid., 163). High trust systems encourage deepening the culture of trust, and using situational pressures to learn and grow.

Employees will feel the impact of situational pressures in a variety of ways. In a high capacity system that is continually evolving and asking people to give their best, people can become change weary. Better to proactively prevent change fatigue, rather than deal with it after the fact. At a minimum, leaders can encourage well-being practices and celebration of accomplished goals to renew coworker energy. Another potential impact is chaos and confusion if poor communication habits take root. Since high trust systems are held together through positive relationships and collaborative teams, clear ongoing communication is necessary for people to work well together.

A positive impact happens if the fulfillment of personal purpose aligns with organizational purpose; this gives employees a great opportunity to use their gifts and talents toward something that matters deeply to them. People have a strong willingness to contribute when they share common interests and they see the benefits of working together. Willingness is cultivated by creating a climate of trust, honesty, and transparency; where mutual support and relationships are a priority; and where establishing a sense of community and belonging is central. Situational pressures create the opportunity for people to work together toward something they care about with people they care about.

As described earlier, high-control systems use hierarchical structure and task-orientation to manage operations and assess quality. Noted in Chapter 5, this type of system has difficulty adapting to environmental pressures. By contrast, high trust systems cultivate positive relationships and collaborative team dynamics to achieve organizational goals. Mutual trust rather than directed control is the element that holds this type of system together during difficult times. The aim of this chapter was to illustrate the interconnections of conflict, power, and organizational change in two different climates using a framework of the three crucial arenas of organizational involvement. The hope is that questions and insights have been raised for critical reflection regarding your own context.

References

Barrett, Richard. 2017. *The Values-Driven Organization.* 2nd ed. New York: Routledge.

Bolman, Lee G., and Terrence E. Deal. 2017. *Reframing Organizations: Artistry, Choice, and Leadership.* 6th ed. Hoboken: Wiley.

Bridges, William, and Susan Bridges. 2017. *Managing Transitions: Making the Most of Change.* 25th Anni. ed. Boston: Da Capo Lifelong Books.

Buono, Anthony F., and Kenneth W. Kerber. 2010. "Creating a Sustainable Approach to Change: Building Organizational Change Capacity." *SAM Advanced Management Journal* 75 (2): 4–21.

Colwill, Deborah A. 2005. "Dialogical Learning and a Renewed Epistemology: Analysis of Cultural and Educational Shifts from Modernity toward Postmodernity." PhD diss., Trinity International University.

———. 2010. "The Use of Metaphor in Consulting for Organizational Change." In *Consultation for Organizational Change.* Edited by Anthony F. Buono and David W. Jamieson, 113–35. Charlotte: Information Age Publishing.

Cooperrider, David L., Diana Whitney, Jacqueline M. Stavros, and Ronald Fry. 2008. *The Appreciative Inquiry Handbook: For Leaders of Change.* 2nd ed. Brunswick: Berrett-Koehler Publishers.

DePree, Max. 2003. *Leading Without Power: Finding Hope in Serving Community.* San Francisco: Jossey-Bass.

DeRue, D. Scott, and Kristina M. Workman. 2013. "Toward a Positive and Dynamic Theory of Leadership Development." In *The Oxford Handbook of Positive Organizational Scholarship.* Edited by Kim S. Cameron and Gretchen M. Spreitzer, 784–97. New York: Oxford University Press.

Edmondson, Amy C. 2019. *The Fearless Organization: Creating Psychological Safety in the Workplace for Learning, Innovation, and Growth.* Hoboken: Wiley.

Fairholm, Gilbert W. 2009. *Organizational Power Politics: Tactics in Organizational Leadership.* 2nd ed. Santa Barbara: Praeger.

Follett, Mary Parker. 1924. *Creative Experience.* New York: Longmans, Green & Co.

———. [1925] 2013. *Dynamic Administration: The Collected Papers of Mary Parker Follett.* Mansfield Centre: Martino Fine Books.

Hardy, Cynthia. 1996. "Understanding Power: Bringing about Strategic Change." *British Journal of Management* 7 (1): S3–16. https://doi.org/10.1111/j.1467-8551.1996.tb00144.x

Hicks, Donna. 2019. *Leading with Dignity: How to Create a Culture That Brings Out the Best in People.* Reprint ed. New Haven: Yale University Press.

Hill, Linda A., Greg Brandeau, Emily Truelove, and Kent Lineback. 2014. *Collective Genius: The Art and Practice of Leading Innovation.* Boston: Harvard Business Review Press.

Hughes, Mark. 2019. *Managing and Leading Organizational Change.* New York: Routledge.

Isaacs, William. 1999. *Dialogue: The Art of Thinking Together.* New York: Currency.

Komives, Susan R., and Wendy Wagner, eds. 2017. *Leadership for a Better World: Understanding the Social Change Model of Leadership Development.* 2nd ed. San Francisco: Jossey-Bass.

Kouzes, James M., and Barry Z. Posner. 2016. *Learning Leadership: The Five Fundamentals of Becoming an Exemplary Leader.* Hoboken: Wiley.

———. 2017. *The Leadership Challenge: How to Make Extraordinary Things Happen in Organizations.* 6th ed. Hoboken: Wiley.

McCauley, Cynthia D., D. Scott DeRue, Paul R. Yost, and Sylvester Taylor. 2013. *Experience-Driven Leader Development: Models, Tools, Best Practices, and Advice for On-the-Job Development.* 3rd ed. San Francisco: Jossey-Bass.

McGregor, Douglas. [1960] 2006. *The Human Side of Enterprise.* Annotated ed. New York: McGraw-Hill.

Mintzberg, Henry. 1983. *Power in and Around Organizations.* Englewood Cliffs: Pearson.

Quinn, Robert E. 2000. *Change the World: How Ordinary People Can Achieve Extraordinary Results.* San Francisco: Jossey-Bass.

Quinn, Robert E., and Gretchen M. Spreitzer. 1997. "The Road to Empowerment: Seven Questions Every Leader Should Consider." *Organizational Dynamics* 26 (2): 37–49. https://doi.org/10.1016/S0090-2616(97)90004-8

Raines, Susan S. 2020. *Conflict Management for Managers: Resolving Workplace, Client, and Policy Disputes.* 2nd ed. Lanham: Rowman & Littlefield Publishers.

Schein, Edgar H., and Peter A. Schein. 2017. *Organizational Culture and Leadership.* 5th ed. Hoboken: Wiley.

———. 2018. *Humble Leadership: The Power of Relationships, Openness, and Trust.* Oakland: Berrett-Koehler Publishers.

Schon, Donald A. 1987. *Educating the Reflective Practitioner: Toward a New Design for Teaching and Learning in the Professions.* San Francisco: Jossey-Bass.

Singh, Amarjit. 2009. "Organizational Power in Perspective." *Leadership & Management in Engineering* 9 (4): 165–76. https://doi.org/10.1061/(ASCE)LM.1943-5630.0000018

Snow, Charles C. 2015. "Organizing in the Age of Competition, Cooperation, and Collaboration." *Journal of Leadership & Organizational Studies* 22 (4): 433–42. https://doi.org/10.1177/1548051815585852

Spreitzer, Gretchen M. 2006. "Leadership Development Lessons from Positive Organizational Studies." *Organizational Dynamics* 35 (4): 305–15. https://doi.org/10.1016/j.orgdyn.2006.08.005

Index

Note: Page locators in **bold** indicate a table on the corresponding page.

Printed in the United States
by Baker & Taylor Publisher Services